AF291255

A Cat, a Dog, a Microwave...

Cultural Practices and Politics of Image Datasets

Edited by
Nicolas Malevé
and Ioanna Zouli

On the Photographic Imaginaries of AI: Ioanna Zouli in conversation with Katrina Sluis

In the summer of 2016, Katrina Sluis and Sam Mercer invited me to work together on a project that they were developing at The Photographers' Gallery: the online platform Unthinking Photography. In an inversion of Victor Burgin's 1982 *Thinking Photography*, the title suggested a departure from traditional conceptions, representational systems and cycles of photographic production. It played on new conceptions of photography as "mindless" as a result of its inhuman scale, velocity, automation and proliferation through social networks. The platform became the online voice of the Gallery's Digital Programme, and through commissioned writing, visual essays, art projects and the *imgexhaust* Tumblr, it has been exploring the aesthetics and politics of photographic culture today. Since 2016, the platform has hosted essays and interviews by more than 40 writers, artists, misfits and practitioners.

After five years of online-only presence, this publication is the first print output from Unthinking Photography. It assembles a series of essays that were published online between 2016 and 2020 as well as new, commissioned, texts that serve as a series of provocations concerning the photographic cultures that inform computer vision.

A key strand of Unthinking Photography has focused on demystifying practices of image annotation and the infrastructures of computer vision. It sits in close dialogue with Data/Set/Match, a yearlong programme of commissions and events centred on image datasets and their role in shaping AI imaginaries, which ran at The Photographers' Gallery from 2019-2020.[1] The initiative aimed to draw attention to the uses and politics of images in the computer sciences – connecting the image dataset to photographic discourse. Unthinking Photography has become an archive of this programme, as well as the various collaborations the Gallery's digital team initiated over this period.

The speed at which technology develops, algorithms mutate, and ideas circulate in networked spaces is often asymmetrical to the pace in which cultural organisations produce work about these ecologies. So, this book marks a moment in – technological, historical – time when knowledge about visual datasets was created and circulated beyond the discipline of computer science, and considered from the perspective of the cultural institution. A moment of consideration

---

1   *Data/Set/Match* ran at The Photographers' Gallery Media Wall and online from 1 April 2019 to 31 October 2020. Specifically, it included the following commissions: *Exhibiting ImageNet* by Nicolas Malevé, *How Do You See me?* by Heather Dewey-Hagborg, *The Future is Here!* by Mimi Onuoha, *Laws of Ordered Form* by Anna Ridler, *Declassifier* by Philipp Schmitt, *A Kitchen of One's Own* by xtine burrough and Sabrina Starnaman, *Lacework* by Everest Pipkin. Due to the restrictions of the Covid-19 pandemic in 2020, the Gallery commissioned online iterations of the works by Schmitt, burrough and Starnaman, and Pipkin. The first year of the programme included a symposium at The Photographers' Gallery looking at 'What does the dataset want?' (14 September 2019). As an extension of the symposium activities, the Gallery celebrated the 10th anniversary of ImageNet with a Birthday Party and Guest of Honour: its creator, Dr. Fei-Fei Li. The programme culminated with an online roundtable discussion that focused on the topic of 'Working with datasets' (15 October 2020).

of how art can address computer vision and how an art institution can stage cross-disciplinary discussions about the role of algorithmic technologies in the formation of image culture.

It is also important to situate this publication in the context of the work of the Digital Programme team at The Photographers' Gallery, and the collaborations and reflexive practices that developed over the years. I, therefore, invited Katrina Sluis[2] to an in-conversation[3] about the origins of the Digital Programme, its exhibition practices and how they developed over time, as well as how practices of computer vision and its paradigms are important in understanding contemporary visual literacy.

Ioanna Zouli: Could you start by telling us a bit about your work as a Digital Curator at The Photographers' Gallery and the context under which the Digital Programme emerged at the institution?

Katrina Sluis: The Gallery's Digital Programme was established in 2012 in response to the tsunami of bastardised, semi-automated, networked images resulting from the convergence of camera, phone and internet, which seemed to challenge established ideas of "the pho-

---

2   Katrina Sluis is presently Adjunct Research Curator at The Photographers' Gallery. She was appointed as the first Digital Curator at The Photographers' Gallery in 2011. Jon Uriarte has taken up the post from 2019, working with Sam Mercer who has been Digital Producer and Assistant Curator from 2014.

3   The conversation took place over Zoom in April 2021, in different time zones, in the middle of the global Covid-19 pandemic. It was recorded and then transcribed by Trint's software algorithms and edited with the human interventions of Ioanna and Katrina.

tographer" and the role of a photography institution. It was an interesting time to be launching such an initiative in Britain. At a point where photography had finally entered the canon of art and achieved market success, network culture was assaulting the values on which this status had been secured. With the support of the Esmeé Fairbairn Foundation, the Gallery created the new post of Digital Curator to help them navigate these issues. By the time I was appointed, the decision had been made to install a permanent digital exhibition space on the ground floor of its refurbished building, which was re-opened in 2012. The resulting technical solution, an 8 panel Media Wall, connected the Gallery to the ecosystem of screens that populated the stores of nearby Oxford Street and Piccadilly Circus. Clearly visible from the street, the Media Wall announced the Gallery's intention to explore different systems of image circulation and display.

Despite its limitations as a platform, the Media Wall was mobilised as a tool for playfully contaminating the institution with different kinds of image cultures and practices. The inaugural project *Born in 1987: The Animated GIF* (2012), arose from a desire to address the cultural dynamics of image diffusion and hyper-circulation. In celebrating an image file format, we tried to counter the fetishisation of the "pictorial" which underpins 20th century photographic scholarship and draw attention to the aesthetic brilliance of the network "user". In this respect, the programme has been informed by the agenda of software studies, in which technology is positioned not just as a "tool" but also as politics and culture.

Almost a decade later, this concern is evident in major projects such as Data/Set/Match (2019-2020) which, from an institutional perspective, sought to position the computer scientist as increasingly entailed in the creation and curation of photographic culture, and the image dataset as a significant cultural form requiring public interrogation. Today, the Digital Programme is led by Jon Uriarte, in collaboration with Sam Mercer: two brilliant colleagues whose curatorial expertise has been crucial in pushing Data/Set/Match into new directions and whose vision continues to shape the ambitions of the programme.

IZ   In an interview from 2012 published by Furtherfield,[4] you mentioned how the programme was motivated by a need "to rethink familiar notions of photography and temporality, indexicality and the economy of the image – concerns which presently haunt the field of photography theory". How easy do you think it was for photographic institutions at the time to address this need? And how did the programme attempt to bridge the space between photography theory and networked art practices?

KS   The problem, of course, is that in photography institutions, the curator's conventional role is to valorise photographic representation, develop a canon of artists and materialise exhibitions of "photographs" for its walls. However, this ignores the problem that in a screen-based photographic culture, contemporary photography is a software performance, or – following Andrew Dewdney and Anne-Marie Willis – an apparition or "zom-

4   Garrett, M. (2012) 'An interview with Katrina Sluis, Digital Curator at the Photographers' Gallery', *Furtherfield*. Available at: https://www.furtherfield.org/an-interview-with-katrina-sluis-digital-curator-at-the-photographers-gallery/ (Accessed 1 July 2021).

bie" who refuses to die, destined to terrorise our devices as data displayed in the culturally received form of a photograph.[5] In this sense, of course, photography is the outcome of a socio-technical performance that does not even have to originate in a human photographer anymore. In an age of the "redundant photographer", there was a unique opportunity for The Photographers' Gallery to interrogate the values on which it was founded.[6] It is clear, now more than ever, that photography is a collaborative act of humans and nonhumans; of software, bodies, machines and networks.

In the early years the programme had a definite focus on the aesthetics and politics of image circulation. Our 2012 Media Wall project *For the LOL of Cats: Felines, Photography and the Web* playfully unpacked the cat-industrial-complex, drawing on the expertise of online cat photography curators whilst highlighting the agency of the nonhuman (cat) photographer. Through a project like this, we were able to smuggle in critical debates at that time around the attention economy and communicative capitalism.[7] As the programme continued, further questions emerged. For example, how can we be-

5   Dewdney, A. (2021) *Forget Photography,* London: Goldsmiths UP and Willis, A. -M. (1990) 'Digitisation and the Living Death of Photography', in Hayward, P. (ed.) *Culture, Technology & Creativity in the Late Twentieth Century.* London: John Libbey.

6   See for example Palmer, D (2013). 'Redundant photographs: cameras, software and human obsolescence', in: Rubinstein, D., Golding, J., & Fisher, A. (Eds.), *On the Verge of Photography: Imaging Beyond Representation.* Birmingham: ARTicle Press, pp. 49 - 67.

7   A selected set of commissioned essays from this project have been reproduced on Unthinking Photography. Please see: https://unthinking. photography/themes/cat-photography.

gin to talk about photographic representation as being operationalised or cannibalised by computational systems? How can you begin to make projects which talk about photography as a process, not an object?

IZ I like the idea of thinking of photography as a process and not just an object – on the one hand because it's challenging the traditional concept of the museum as the guardian of material culture, and on the other, because it leaves space to consider that, in the networked environment, the photographic practice is not necessarily performed by one person – the photographer – but can be defined by many different agents, both human and nonhuman. Did this processual dimension influence the way that you curated the Media Wall exhibitions and the programme in general?

KS For those of us working on the Digital Programme, it has been important to emphasise that photographic culture is now being sustained by a variety of agents who sit outside the traditional scope of cultural institutions – I'm thinking here of the computer scientist, web designer, Silicon Valley entrepreneur or Amazon Mechanical Turker. And of course, these are actors who are not engaged with photographic culture and the politics of representation, the history of photography or the inherent polysemy of the image. In the computer science lab, the photograph remains relatively uncomplicated – it is ultimately a blob of information – whether materialised as a "picture" or left latent as data.

In this sense, the historical methods through which the humanities approach the image and its various meaning(s) are now eclipsed by the paradigm of pattern and randomness. As scholar Martin Lister has proposed, cybernetic logic replaces signifier and signified.[8] This represents a very interesting shift because, of course, it demands a different set of approaches. It challenges certain sectors of humanities who can't see beyond the glittering photographic surfaces of the camera-phone, for whom computation is "immaterial". It also challenges the computer scientists who position the photograph as a neutral and transparent carrier of data. And it challenges The Photographers' Gallery and others who champion visual literacy because it demands a different set of skills, expertise and pedagogy.

Faced with the scale and velocity of image culture, the answer of many in the photographic community has been to fetishise "slow looking", in which the essence of the jpeg might reveal itself through a form of committed hyper-semiology. In contrast, the Digital Programme has tried to offer up a series of projects that have sought to increase knowledge and public understanding of the conditions of photographic ubiquity, automation and machine vision. This work is referenced by Nicolas Malevé later in this volume, recognising that in computer vision "seeing" is operationalised as a millisecond glance. [see pp.141-167]

IZ Can you say a bit more about these projects and your curatorial approach?

---

8   See Lister, M. (2007) 'A Sack in the Sand: Photography in the Age of Information', *Convergence: The International Journal of Research into New Media Technologies*, 13(3), pp. 251-274. doi: 10.1177/1354856507079176.

KS Many institutions have embraced computer vision technologies as a tool for creating novel interfaces for their digitised collections and extracting new knowledge from them. As a photo institution operating on a Kunsthalle model, we instead position it as a socio-technical cultural form and fundamentally photographic project, grounded in the labour of the amateur photographer, photo sharing platforms, and the imaginaries of the photographic archive. This approach has informed a number of initiatives which include artistic commissions, public programmes and university partnerships.

In opening up a discussion on machine ways of seeing, from 2014 we commissioned and exhibited further works by the Scandinavian Institute of Computational Vandalism, Paolo Cirio and Alessandro Ludovico, Erica Scourti, ScanLAB Projects and James Bridle. In 2016 we commissioned Sebastian Schmieg to develop a new work in his *Search by Image* series for the Media Wall, focusing on the image processing "test image" Lena.jpg. This was accompanied by a further online commission, *Decision Space*, which turned visitors to The Photographers' Gallery website into image annotators, and created a conceptual machine learning dataset which Sebastian exhibited in 2017 with the title *This is the Problem, the Solution, the Past and the Future*. He discusses this project in more detail with Nicolas Malevé later in this volume. [see pp.75-88]

Recognising a need to transform photographic pedagogy and public understanding of computer vision, we ran an "Experimental Photo School" in 2017 and 2018 which included workshops addressing automation, coding and speculative machine learning for photographers. This built on our 2016 Robot Vision Geekender which had live events, talks and performances that focused on the camera as a "seeing machine".[9]

Around this time, we had many frustrated photography students from London art schools attending these programmes. They complained that their reading lists would end in the 1980s with Victor Burgin's writing, and they would be left in class to ponder what theorists like Susan Sontag would think of Google Street View. This informed our decision to commission accessible writing around the programme, and launch the online platform Unthinking Photography in 2016. This was also the year we commissioned Geoff Cox's essay *Ways of Machine Seeing* which has been one of the most popular texts and is reproduced later in this volume.

But perhaps most significantly, we developed a collaborative PhD with the Centre for the Study of the Networked Image at London South Bank University and appointed Nicolas Malevé. From 2016-2020 Nicolas researched what it means to think about photography and machine vision from the position of the person who annotates images industrially. As part of this work, Nicolas began re-staging a 2007 experiment conducted by Dr Fei-Fei Li, Pietro Perona, Christof Koch and Asha Iyer that studied what can be perceived from a scene in a glance, and informed the development of ImageNet – a key da-

9   On Seeing Machines, see Paglen, T. (2014) 'Is Photography Over?', *Still Searching: Fotomuseum Winterthur*. Available at: https://www.fotomuseum.ch/de/series/is-photography-over/ (Accessed 22 July 2021).

taset in computer vision.[10] Nicolas re-enacts this experiment in order to ask what kind of vision informs these systems; what kind of photography is used and generated in these conditions, and how does this impact on the way machines see the world? This "re-experiment" has been conducted with gallery staff, members of the public, and, ultimately with Dr Fei-Fei Li herself at the Gallery in 2019.

In his thesis Nicolas makes the case for the photographic institution as a site where the "experimental" apparatuses of computer vision can be questioned and engaged with, in ways that are not possible within the narrow margins of the lab. But he argues this can only happen if the institution conceives its role not exclusively in terms of an art institution, but as a site where different "alignments of practices, devices and ways of seeing coming and going under the name photography can be explored in their active role in the modelling of the technologies of vision".[11]

10   Fei-Fei, L. et al. (2007) 'What do we perceive in a glance of a real-world scene?', *Journal of Vision*, 7(1), p. 10. doi: 10.1167/7.1.10.

11   Malevé, N. (2021) *Algorithms of Vision. Human and machine learning in computational visual culture*. PhD thesis. London South Bank University.

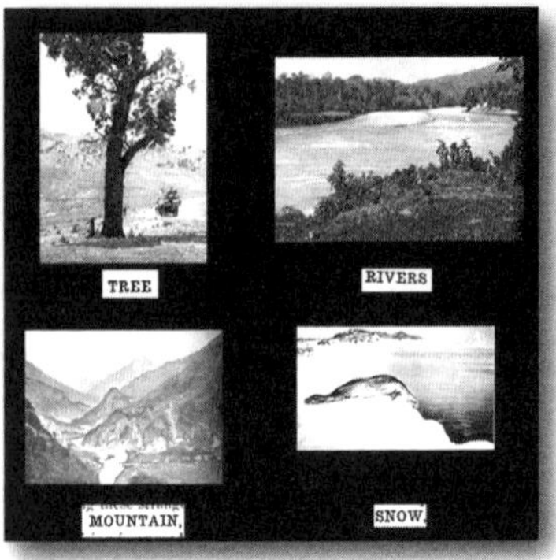

Still from Anna Ridler's *Laws of Ordered Form*, presented on TPG Media Wall in 2020 as part of the Data/Set/Match programme.

IZ What do you think the photo institution learnt from the Data/Set/Match programme?

KS Data/Set/Match was a curatorial initiative that tried to pivot the institution away from the paradigm of aesthetic modernism in order to grasp photography as an unimaginable, insane, socio-technical system that literally covers the globe and involves all of us in processes of extraction and subjectification. In confronting photography at this scale, the dataset became a concrete site, which one can actually materialise and collectively interrogate. The dataset escapes the abstract totality of "the algorithm", and connects with issues of labour, identity, knowledge, circulation and control continuous with histories of the photographic archive. Perhaps, most crucially, the dataset is where you see that AI is a fundamentally photographic project – one which cannot sidestep older histories of image classification, categorisation, taxonomy and bias.

See IMG 1 on page 176

IZ Data/Set/Match launched with the project *Exhibiting ImageNet* – an experiment that was devised in collaboration with Nicolas Malevé and displayed on the gallery's Media Wall from July 2019 to September 2019. Could you briefly introduce us to this dataset and to its role in image classification practices?

KS ImageNet has become the canonical dataset on which much of the discussion of politics of datasets and machine learning centres.[12] ImageNet is a huge semantic machine; a feat of engineering that has brought together computer scientists, linguists, search engine algorithms, Flickr photographers, 25,000 Amazon Mechanical Turkers, to collectively produce a visual map of the world as identifiable objects. In this way, ImageNet sits alongside other historical attempts at other taxonomic projects that have been extensively theorised in photography: from Aby Warburg's *Mnemosyne* and Malraux's *Le Musée imaginaire* to Edward Steichen's *The Family of Man*; commercial databases such as Getty images, Corbis; to the colonial, medical and military photographic archives held by the state. Data/Set/Match became an initiative through which contemporary computer vision and histories of photography could come into contact, creating transdisciplinary discussions.

---

12 See in particular the important work of artist and researcher Adam Harvey, including https://www.vframe.io/ and exposing.ai. Read more at: https://ahprojects.com/.

But perhaps most significantly, the dataset also leads us back to the imaging practices of the computer lab, which – in its own way – is highly fascinating and politically charged. On the one hand, you have the University of Edinburgh[13] marshalling troupes of ceilidh dancers to be recorded overhead for the sole purpose of capturing structured motion behaviour. On the other hand, you have the scraping of millions of online holiday photos, celebrity pics and other "images in the wild". There is obviously much to unpack between these two poles, as this volume demonstrates. One begins to see how the photographic practices of the computer sciences – like those of the photo museum – have been transformed by network culture.

IZ Of course it has also transformed the photographic practices of professional and amateur photographers, who found in the network a space to share, archive and reproduce their images. I know that you have done extensive research on Flickr not only as a photo-sharing platform, but also as one of the main websites that were used for the construction of large visual datasets such as ImageNet, through extreme image scraping. Would you like to discuss the impact of networked photographic practices and their relation to datasets?

KS Recent advances in computer vision have been reliant on the emergence of social media and the accessibility of user generated content. In a series of articles for Fotomuseum Winterthur's *Still Search-*

---

13 See, for example: Edinburgh Ceilidh Overhead Video Data. Available at: https://homepages.inf.ed.ac.uk/rbf/CEILIDHDATA/ (Accessed 22 July 2021).

ing platform, I have described how computer vision heavily relies on the labour of amateur photographers.[14] ImageNet is a snapshot of Flickr from around 2008. Computer scientists have turned to websites like photo.net and dpreview.com as sources of training data for the aesthetic evaluation of images. Datasets such as AVA are made up from images and community rankings harvested from these amateur photo communities. These become the "ground truth" on which machines learn what a beautiful – and therefore successful – image might look like.

These machine learning systems now find their way into mobile photo platforms such as EyeEm and VSCO. Marketed variously as AI or "on demand curation", these systems help photographers optimise their output and choose which images to share. This generates a strange situation where the aesthetic values of amateur photographers are used to train an algorithm. At the same time, through such interfaces they are positioned as an audience to be aesthetically disciplined, in need of guidance or training in what makes a beautiful image. It creates what I describe as an "aesthetic bubble": a recursive system where the amateur photographer is simultaneously both a source of photographic expertise, and deficient in photographic knowledge.

See IMG 2 on page 177

14   Sluis, K. (2019) 'Photography must be curated!' *Still Searching: Fotomuseum Winterthur*. Available at: https://www.fotomuseum.ch/en/series/photography-must-be-curated/ (Accessed 22 July 2021).

IZ I find it extremely interesting how you managed to bring these networked qualities of the image into the Gallery through the context of the dataset. Also, what I still find striking is how you displayed 14,197,122 (!) photographs from ImageNet on the Media Wall – so as soon as a visitor entered the Gallery they would be flooded with images at a really fast speed. Considering the more traditional display conditions of the photograph as a singular material object in museums or photo institutions, exhibiting a whole visual dataset in the gallery proposes such a different scale of working with, and looking at, images in the context of a cultural organisation. How did you approach matters of scale in this project?

KS Whilst computer science seeks to solve the problem of photographic scale, it's important to also recognise that the Gallery is not immune to problems of scale. Although – if the proliferation of singular, enframed, discrete photographs in museums is anything to go by – it pretends to be. Whilst problematic in many ways, the Media Wall offered a unique platform through which to experiment with the scale of the networked image via the dataset. One of the key issues is that ImageNet, as a dataset of 14 million images, is difficult to "see" in its entirety, and presents itself differently if you spend time scrolling through the images that define the synsets that define "cake", "woman" or "semite".[15] One begins to witness both the scale of the training data

15 Malevé, N. (2020) 'On the data set's ruins', *AI & Society*, 36, pp. 1117-1131, https://doi.org/10.1007/s00146-020-01093-w.

and its classificatory infrastructure. When we invited Fei-Fei Li to the Gallery to discuss the creation of ImageNet in a public forum, she was surprised that we had taken the time to look at the dataset and pay attention to the individual images.

So the question of how to exhibit 14 million images became a critical gesture and experiment. *Exhibiting ImageNet* took over the Media Wall for a period of two months, at a rate of 40 milliseconds per image, and is discussed later in this book. The curatorial approach echoed the speed of perception that Fei-Fei Li set up in the Caltech experiment we had been performing in the Gallery. The display was also organised by synset,[16] which was overlaid in the feed. This sought to emphasise the underlying image-language problem and the underlying infrastructure of WordNet on which its ontology is based. This was a different approach to Trevor Paglen, whose project *From Apple to Anomaly* reproduced 30,000 printed images from ImageNet at the Barbican later that year.[17]

IZ As part of that season you also staged a 10th birthday party for ImageNet. Playful and somewhat celebratory, what was the rationale behind this event?

KS The gesture of staging an ImageNet birthday party was both a provocation and a pragmatic gesture to attract a world leading computer scientist – Fei-Fei

---

16 A set of synonyms and a category in the WordNet jargon. For more on Wordnet's lexical database see Fellbaum, C. (ed.) (1998) *WordNet: an electronic lexical database*, Cambridge, MA: MIT Press.

17 Learn more about Trevor Paglen's project here: https://www.barbican. org.uk/whats-on/2019/event/trevor-paglen-from-apple-to-anomaly (Accessed 22 July 2021).

Li – to a mid-sized London gallery. It reflected a sincere attempt to position the dataset not as an object that belongs only to computer science, but as something with a public life, a history, a politics and agency to act in the world – worthy of narration and critical attention. There is an obvious need for more conversations across disciplinary boundaries about the consequences of classification and the politics of representation that datasets are enmeshed in and perpetuate. At a time when important public debates about ImageNet were entering public consciousness,[18] we wanted to create a space where computer scientists, artists, scholars, technologists, photographers and interested members of the public could have an open discussion of the visual dataset, the imaginaries it represents and the problematic view of the world it embodies.[19]

IZ And of course, it's crucial to examine the kind of world that the dataset embodies. What it includes and who or what is kept out from this visual representation of the world. How do you think we can address the biases of the datasets? Was this something that you had in mind when initiating the Data/Set/Match programme?

KS Yes, this was our motivation – anyone who has studied the history of photography understands how the photographic archive is a site of power and classification, which is most clearly seen in facial recognition technologies. Over the same

18   For example Trevor Paglen and Kate Crawford's ImageNet Roulette project of 2019: https://imagenet-roulette.paglen.com.

19   Fei-Fei Li's talk is archived on unthinking.photography: https://unthinking.photography/articles/where-did-imagenet-come-from.

period, there has also been an extremely rich and important body of work emerging from diverse scholarly fields concerning bias in machine learning and how AI systems acquire sexist, racist and other discriminatory qualities.[20] Many critiques tend to focus on datasets, the techno-social infrastructures of machine learning and the models which result. More recently the scholar Olga Goriunova – in an article responding to Fei-Fei Li's talk – has argued that the problem is much larger than labels, categorisation, images and representation. Machine vision limits itself to the horizon of human perception and image-making conventions from the end of the 20th century. She concludes, "the entire field seems to be modeled in a way that has bias at its core."[21]

From here, it becomes clear that the epistemological positions of the computer sciences now contaminate visual culture. At the moment, many web pages that have hosted and disseminated image datasets are being pulled down, revised, and changed. Even finding a complete copy of ImageNet was a difficult technical feat for The Photographers' Gallery. Based on their significance to 21st century visual culture, there is also a case to be

20   See for example the expansive scholarship of Ruha Benjamin, Safiya Umoja Noble, Joy Buolamwini and the Algorithmic Justice League, Timnit Gebru, Meredith Whitaker and the AI Now Institute, Adam Harvey and Jules LaPlace, Abeba Birhane, Catherine D'Ignazio and Lauren F Klein, Louise Amoore, Ramon Amaro, Florian Jaton.

21   Goriunova, O. (2020) 'Humans Categorise Humans: on ImageNet Roulette and Machine Vision', *Donaufestival: Redefining Arts*. Available at: https://pure.royalholloway.ac.uk/portal/files/41356875/ENG_Olga_Goriunova_Human_Categories_DonauFestival_article.pdf (Accessed: 16 July 2021).

made that datasets should be collected and preserved in museum collections.

With this in mind, I think this volume reflects a curiosity about how it is possible to talk about the value and agency of the image in a different way in the photo museum. But as someone who has been working to develop a discourse around these practices, I'm keen to hear more of your reflections on the collected texts, and how we might view them?

IZ This publication is an invitation to consider the role of datasets and the agency of images inhabiting and circulating in online spaces. The collected texts mark a period of discussions in the Digital Programme from 2016 to 2021, with seven of the essays having been previously published online on Unthinking Photography, while three have been commissioned specifically for this print publication.[22] The resulting collection is a series of reflections on visual datasets by artists, theorists, researchers, and curators that work within the orbit of computer science and networked cultures. It draws attention to the labour included in the creation of image datasets, as well as the politics of machine vision and practices that define datasets as a visual project. And I think this brings forward an important point, as you also highlighted in our discussion: that contemporary photographic debates and museum practices should be attentive to

---

22 The newly commissioned essays are: *Working with Datasets* by Jon Uriarte, *About Face: A Survey on Facial Recognition Datasets* by Genevieve Fried and Deborah Raji and *The Age of ImageNet's Discovery* by Alan F. Blackwell.

processes that happen outside the canon of traditional image production and exhibition.

In the summer of 2019 one could walk into The Photographers' Gallery and watch the endless stream of images of *Exhibiting ImageNet* on the Media Wall, then go up the stairs to see an exhibition about Latin American photographers and a group show of artists selected for the TPG New Talent programme. Exhibiting algorithmic processes along with a history of photography in a non-Western geography, as well as with the work of rising practitioners is, for me, a merging of practices that poses a good example of situating an expanded approach to photography inside the museum. In a similar vein, I consider this collection of essays as standing in between disciplines: on the one hand it could be seen next to photo exhibition catalogues, books on photo archives or collections, and on the other next to publications that discuss digital curation or networked art practices.

Also, the period that Nicolas and I spent thinking with this book material coincided with the first year of the global Covid-19 pandemic; a time when the power of the image in its computational and networked form was strongly evident. Images became part of a screen-based sociality during the lockdowns of the first year of Covid, while new machine vision datasets made their appearance to support commercial and scientific needs that occured during this period of crisis. I'm thinking here of the Real-world Masked Face Recognition Dataset or the Public Covid-19 X-ray dataset,[23] for example. I find it extremely interesting how quickly machine vision technologies, and the human and non-human agents behind them, respond and find solutions to new problems that arise. These solutions produce new knowledge, which, in the example of image datasets, is linked to the visual understanding of the world as well as to its representation(s). Considering how rapidly computer vision technologies develop and get applied, critical observation and analysis is important and necessary. The essays included in this book reflect on image datasets as powerful agents of knowledge creation and distribution, looking at matters of access and infrastructure. Adding to that, the artists' works in this volume perceive datasets beyond their instrumentalist role in computer vision, drawing attention to new problems that need critical responses and solutions.

23 You can find out more about these datasets on their dedicated GitHub pages: https://github.com/X-zhangyang/Real-World-Masked-Face-Dataset and https://github.com/v7labs/covid-19-xray-dataset.

Ways of Machine Seeing
Geoff Cox

One of the main questions traversing this publication is what happens to the relation between seeing and knowing within algorithmic procedures? Geoff Cox invites us to look into the apparatuses of vision and pursue the project of political critique inherent to John Berger's *Ways of Seeing* in a reconfigured environment.

You are looking at the front cover of the book *Ways of Seeing*[1] <ℒ1> written by John Berger in 1972. The text is the script of the TV series, and if you've seen the programmes, you can almost hear the distinctive pedagogic tone of Berger's voice as you read his words: "The relation between what we see and what we know is never settled." The image by René Magritte on the cover of the book further emphasises the point about the deep ambiguity of images and the always-present difficulty of legibility between words and seeing.[2]

---

1   The author refers here to the iconic René Magritte's *The Key of Dreams* (1930) featured on Berger's book cover. It represents four pictures paired with words. The discrepancy between the labels and the pictures emphasises the gap between images and their descriptions.

2   Aside from René Magritte's *The Key of Dreams* (1930), Joseph Kosuth's *One and Three Chairs* (1965) comes to mind, which makes a similar point in presenting a chair, a photograph of the chair, and an enlarged dictionary definition of the word "chair". See Wikipedia page: https://en.wikipedia.org/wiki/One_and_Three_Chairs.

In addition to an explicit reference to the work of art by Walter Benjamin,[3] the TV programme employed Brechtian techniques, such as revealing the technical apparatus of the studio, to encourage viewers not to simply watch (or read) in an easy way but rather to be forced into an analysis of elements of "separation" that would lead to a "return from alienation."[4] <🔗2>

Berger further reminded the viewer of the specifics of the technical reproduction in use and its ideological force in a similar manner:

"But remember that I am controlling and using for my own purposes the means of reproduction needed for these programmes [...] with this programme as with all programmes, you receive images and meanings which are arranged. I hope you will consider what I arrange but please remain skeptical of it."[5]

That you are not really looking at the book as such but a scanned image of a book – viewable by means of an embedded link to a server where the image is stored – testifies to the ways in which what, and how, we see and know is further unsettled through complex assemblages of elements. The increasing use of relational machines (such as search engines) is a good example of the ways in which knowledge is filtered at the expense

---

3   The first section of the TV programme and the book is acknowledged to be largely based on Benjamin's essay 'The Work of Art in the Age of Mechanical Reproduction' (1936).

4   You can watch the 4 episodes of the BBC program on YouTube. Available at: https://www.youtube.com/watch?v=0pDE4VX_9Kk (Accessed 22 July 2021).

5   The idea is that "separation" produces a disunity that is disturbing to the viewer/reader – Brecht's "alienation-effect" (Verfremdungeffekt) – and that this leads to a potential "return from alienation".

of the more specific detail on how it was produced. Knowledge is now produced in relation to planetary computational infrastructures in which other agents such as algorithms generalise massive amounts of (big) data. [6] <🔗3>

Clearly algorithms do not act alone or with magical (totalising) power, but exist as part of larger infrastructures and ideologies. Some well-publicised recent cases that have come to public attention exemplify a contemporary politics (and crisis) of representation in this way, such as the Google search results for "three black teenagers" and "three white teenagers" <🔗4> (mug shots and happy teens at play, respectively).[7]

The problem is one of learning in its widest sense; "machine learning" techniques are employed on data to produce forms of knowledge that are inextricably bound to hegemonic systems of power and prejudice.

There is a sense in which the world begins to be reproduced through computational models and algorithmic logic, changing what and how we see, think and even behave. Subjects are produced in relation to what algorithms understand about our intentions, gestures, behaviours, opinions, or desires, through aggregating massive amounts of data (data mining) and machine learning (the predictive practices of data mining).[8]

---

6   To give a sense of scale and its consequences, Facebook has developed the face-recognition software DeepFace. With over 1.5 billion users that have uploaded more than 250 billion photographs, it is allegedly capable of identifying any person depicted in a given image with 97% accuracy.

7   Allen, A. (2016, June 10) 'The "black teenagers" search shows it is society, not Google, that is racist', The Guardian.

8   Mackenzie, A. (2015) 'The Production of Prediction: What Does Machine Learning Want?', *European Journal of Cultural Studies*, 18, 4-5, p. 431.

That machines learn is accounted for through a combination of calculative practices that help to approximate what will likely happen through the use of different algorithms and models. The difficulty lies in determining to what extent these generalisations are accurate, or to what degree the predictive model is valid, or "able to generalise" sufficiently well. Hence the "learners" (machine learning algorithms), although working at the level of generalisation, are also highly contextual and specific to the fields in which they operate, in a coming together of what Adrian Mackenzie calls a "play of truth and falsehood".[9]

Thus what constitutes knowledge can be seen to be controlled and arranged in new ways that invoke Berger's earlier call for scepticism. Antoinette Rouvroy is similarly concerned that algorithms begin to define what counts for knowledge as a further case of subjectivation, as we are unable to substantively intervene in these processes of how knowledge is produced.[10]

Rouvroy's claim is that knowledge is delivered "without truth" through the increasing use of machines that filter it through the use of search engines that have no interest in content as such, or detail on how knowledge is generated. Instead they privilege real-time relational infrastructures that subsume the knowledge of workers and machines into generalised assemblages as

---

9   Mackenzie, 'The Production of Prediction', p. 441.

10   See, for instance, Rouvroy, A. (2011) 'Technology, Virtuality and Utopia: Governmentality in an Age of Autonomous Computing', in M. Hildebrandt and A. Rouvroy (eds) *The Philosophy of Law Meets the Philosophy of Technology: Computing and Transformations of Human Agency*, London: Routledge, pp. 136-157.

techniques of "algorithmic governmentality."[11]

In this sense, the knowledge produced is bound together with systems of power that are more and more visual and hence ambiguous in character. Clearly computers further complicate the field of visuality, and ways of seeing, especially in relation to the interplay of knowledge and power. Aside from the totalising aspects (that I have outlined thus far), there are also significant "points of slippage or instability" of epistemic authority, or what Berger would no doubt identify as the further unsettling of the relations between seeing and knowing. So, if algorithms can be understood as seeing, in what sense do they see, and under what conditions? Algorithms are ideological only inasmuch as they are part of larger infrastructures and assemblages.

But whether machines can see or not is the wrong question to ask; we should rather discuss how machines have changed the nature of seeing and hence our knowledge of the world.[12]

---

11   To use Rouvroy's phrase. This line of argument is also close to what Tiziana Terranova has called an "infrastructure of autonomization", making reference to Marx's views on automation, particularly in his 'Fragment on Machines', as a description of how machines subsume the knowledge and skill of workers into wider assemblages. See, Terranova, T. (2014) Red Stack Attack! Algorithms, capital and the automation of the common, *Effimera* (Accessed 24 August 2020).

12   I take this assertion from Benjamin once more, who considered the question of whether film or photography to be art secondary to the question of how art itself has been radically transformed: "Earlier much futile thought had been devoted to the question of whether photography is an art. The primary question – whether the very invention of photography had not transformed the nature of art – was not raised. Soon the film theoreticians asked the same ill-considered question with regard to film." Benjamin, W. (1936) *The Work of Art in the Age of Mechanical Reproduction*. Available at: https://web.mit.edu/allanmc/www/benjamin.pdf (Accessed 22 July 2021).

We should not try to oppose machine and human seeing but take them to be more thoroughly entangled – a more "posthuman" or "new materialist" position that challenges the onto-epistemological character of seeing, and produces new kinds of knowledge-power that both challenge as well as extend the anthropomorphism of vision and its attachment to dominant forms of rationality. Clearly there are other (nonhuman) perspectives that also illuminate our understanding of the world. This pedagogic (and political) impulse is perfectly in keeping with *Ways of Seeing* and its project of visual literacy.[13]

What is required is an expansion of this ethic to algorithmic literacy to examine how machine vision unsettles the relations between what we see and what we know in new ways.

See IMG 3 on page 178

13 Berger was associated with The Writers and Readers Publishing Cooperative, aiming to "advance the needs of cultural literacy, rather than cater to an 'advanced' [academic] but limited readership" (From the Firm's declaration of intent). In this sense it draws upon the Marxist cultural materialism of Raymond Williams and Richard Hoggart's *The Uses of Literacy* (1966).

Hyperlinks

<&1>   https://en.wikipedia.org/
        wiki/Ways_of_Seeing
<&2>   https://en.wikipedia.org/
        wiki/Distancing_effect
<&3>   https://research.facebook.com/
        publications/deepface-closing-the-
        gap-to-human-level-performance-
        in-face-verification/
<&4>   https://www.theguardian.com/
        commentisfree/2016/jun/10/three-
        black-teenagers-google-racist-tweet

Working with Datasets
Jon Uriarte

This text is an edited version of the introduction to the online event 'Working with Datasets' that took place on the 15th October 2020, which concluded the year-long Data/Set/Match programme. To contextualise the project, Jon Uriarte, the event's host and moderator, drew a map of the different agents engaged in the production and maintenance of a dataset.

With Data/Set/Match The Photographers' Gallery Digital Programme aimed to explore new ways to present, visualise and interrogate contemporary image datasets by looking into the cultural, political and social impact of these collections of images. Tonight's guest speakers[1] are artists and researchers who have worked with datasets. Some have created them from scratch; others have performed annotating experiments or watched a whole visual dataset with their own eyes. A few have tried to see *as* an algorithm to understand what and how it sees. Other guests have transformed, repurposed or confronted a dataset with other collections of data to look for new and experimental meanings. Ultimately, all of them have critically looked into the impact datasets have in our everyday lives. To start identifying potential directions that a

---

1   The event 'Working with Datasets' was an online roundtable discussion with Philipp Schmitt, xtine burrough, Sabrina Starnaman, Everest Pipkin, Ramon Amaro, Nicolas Malevé, Anna Ridler and moderated by Jon Uriarte.

discussion of their work could take, I will draw a picture of the chain of actors and actions that are key to the creation of visual datasets as well as to their political and cultural dimensions.

So, *who is working with datasets? How do dataset workers carry out their work? Which processes are they involved in, and what is the impact of their work?*
Throughout photography's history, taxonomies have regularly been used to organise and make sense of collections of images. Over the last few decades, the processes of categorisation of photographs have increasingly influenced how machines and humans see and understand the world. Image datasets are collections of images used to train, test and evaluate the performance of an algorithm. In the same way an illustrated book is used to teach children to identify a ball, a dog or a cat, an image dataset usually contains a large number of labelled images that teach algorithms how to identify and name objects in the world.

Scale plays a very relevant role in the way a machine learns. Algorithms trained with large datasets perform much better than those trained with smaller ones. The more annotated and organised photographs in the dataset, the better the conditions of their training and the higher the potential quality of their learning. This relationship consequently increases the number of agents involved. Agents that are usually hidden behind an image of clean, human-less, objective and efficient automation. An image that has recently started to crack, showing that machine learning is not clean; rather, it involves a lot of human labour, and can be inaccurate. There is no such thing as unbiased technology.

In order to identify who is working with datasets, we could start by thinking of all the people whose bodies have been photographed and later unwillingly scraped from the internet to train an algorithm. Even if they weren't aware of it, the representation of their bodies has been used for algorithmic purposes. Photography's traditional ability to erase the agency of the portrayed subjects is increased here even further. A photograph may not only be misinterpreted by a given person at a certain moment, but it may also be pinned with a category and a label, which can easily be offensive and humiliating. This same categorisation is used as input to train a machine how to see the world.

The same goes for the social network users whose photographs are usually scraped from the internet without permission or acknowledgment. Their images are downloaded, repurposed and resignified without retribution. These images stand on their own, without any reference to the person who uploaded them, the platform in which they were published or the interactions that they might have provoked. At the same time, the value that these images generate for the owners of the social media platform in which they were first published is further expanded into other spaces of production: namely, networked spaces that ultimately (re)fuel the attention economy and surveillance capitalism.

The discussion can now move forward to the annotators, who are certainly the biggest group of people working with datasets. As I explained earlier, the ability of the algorithm to recognise, identify or generate an image is closely linked to the size of the dataset. Computer scientists have found that the gig economy provides the perfect companion to accomplish an enormous task that would otherwise easily take more than a lifetime. It allows them to hire a huge workforce to annotate and categorise very large quantities of photographs in a very short time, under precarious conditions, and in exchange for a very modest amount of money. While some of the most powerful industries, including the autonomous car industry, depend on this workforce, the outsourced and crowdsourced workers are hidden and struggle to unionise.

The next focus in my enquiry into the agents working with image datasets is the computer scientists. In the examined context, computer scientists are people who usually lead the projects that create new datasets. They understand photography and images as transparent entities that they rely on to describe the world to machines. They are usually in charge of creating the categories, approving the labelling, as well as training and testing the algorithm against the dataset. These computer scientists – who are, according to demographics, usually white men living in the US – are responsible for the creation and deployment of the dataset and its inevitable bias.

Next, I would like to consider the automated agent of the chain: the algorithm itself. The algorithm could be understood as a recipe that, depending on the ingredients (the dataset), will produce one dish or another as an output. Although it can be tempting to think this 'cooking' is a fully automated process, the reality is that human agents also take part by tweaking its parameters to refine the process, and by choosing the preferred output. However, the algorithm will still only learn from what is in the dataset. Therefore, it will always inherit, and thus reflect, the limitations of trying to describe the world with images. Almost at the end of the chain, we can find the entrepreneur who decides to invest in the development of a visual dataset. The investors may or may not be interested in the conditions under which the work is done; however, being in charge of its deployment, they will definitely be interested in the results and the profits that this work generates.

Finally, if we think of the people actively using the algorithms that were trained with visual datasets, we would probably find the same people whose photographs were used to create the datasets in the first place, without even being aware of the closed circuit in which they participate.

One of the most important issues that emerges from this brief account is how disconnected all these agents are. How their experiences of working with datasets are not shared between them, and how they don't question each other. How crowdworkers are hired through online marketplaces that sit between them and the computer scientists, making it hard to even know who they are working for, and the purpose of their work. How uncritically computer scientists create and deploy visual datasets, treating images as transparent objects without questioning their impact. How the technologists and entrepreneurs go even further, exploiting precarious labour to create new tools – resulting in more bias and discrimination just to make a profit. Finally, how the people whose photographs are being used to create the datasets are not even aware that they were working with datasets in the first place, but are nevertheless subjected to the algorithms trained with their images.

So, again, *who is working with datasets?*

About Face: A Survey
of Facial Recognition Datasets

Genevieve Fried
and Deborah Raji

Genevieve Fried and Deborah Raji offer an historical overview of datasets used in face recognition. Utilising research material gathered through a survey of 100 face datasets, they trace their evolution from snapshot photography to the networked image. Due to the ethical and technical challenges posed by facial recognition systems, dataset evaluation is proposed as a juncture at which transparency and accountability should be provided.

Of the many technologies built using artificial intelligence (AI) methods, perhaps none have provoked as visceral of a reaction as facial processing technology (FPT). FPT, known colloquially as facial recognition, describes the class of algorithms that seek to identify and characterise the facial image of a human subject. The objective is to characterise or identify humans using not much more than their face. The technology is incredibly widespread and omnipresent, impacting millions in airports <𝒫1>, retail stores <𝒫2>, schools <𝒫3>, and even those just walking in the street <𝒫4>. Most recently, this technology is being used for anything from authenticating identities in online proctoring <𝒫5>, to tenant surveillance <𝒫6>, to processing security footage for the police <𝒫7>.

While developers have increasingly inflated the promise of facial recognition with claims of human-level <🔗8> accuracy <🔗9>, researchers have highlighted that the reality is more nuanced and less promising. Many real <🔗10> world <🔗11> pilots of these systems reveal dismal results and perform disproportionately worse <🔗12> on certain under-represented populations.

Facial processing technology involves any task related to the identification and characterisation of the face image of a human subject. This includes *face detection* – the task of locating a face within a bounding box in an image; *face verification* – a one-to-one confirmation that a given photo of an unlabeled face matches another single photo of a known identity; *face identification* – the one-to-many matching of a given image of a face against a database of known images of faces, and *facial analysis* – a classification task to determine facial characteristics, including physical or demographic traits like age, gender or pose, as well as more situational traits such as facial expression. FPT typically uses machine learning, a subset of artificial intelligence algorithms that learn how to act in the world from data. Machine learning models are shaped by the data we feed it, so the type of data we feed our model shapes its objectives. We measure our progress towards these objectives using evaluation metrics. This means that as tasks (i.e. the objective of a machine learning model) evolve over time, so do the data as a representation of the goals of the AI system.

Even though there can be many ways to map out the journey of how FPT has arrived at its present form, one particularly vibrant historical record lies in the evolution of image datasets of human faces used to train, test, and evaluate FPT systems over time. For our 2020 research paper on facial recognition evaluation,[1] we therefore surveyed[2] over 100 facial image datasets constructed between 1976 to 2019. The datasets included more than 145 million images and 17 million subjects culled from a range of sources and contexts. Carefully reading through the source material, we were able to extract and record information on key attributes for each dataset to get a sense of the overall trends in the development of datasets for facial recognition tasks. We found that several key details – from data sources, collection methods, to annotations and distribution practices – change over time in ways worth paying attention to and becoming more conscientious about.

In order to organise our survey, we defined four periods marked by key algorithmic and dataset developments that we felt were critical junctures for FPT development. Period I is marked by the first dataset in our survey; this dates back to 1964 when mathematician and computer scientist Woodrow Bledsoe <🔗13>, funded by an "undisclosed intelligence agency", built a digital dataset of mugshots to attempt <🔗14> to introduce "facial recognition" by a machine for the first time. From there, the creation of the *Face Recognition Technology* (FERET <🔗15>) database in 1996 ushered in Period II. FERET was the very first large-scale face dataset available for academic and commercial research, based on

---

1   Raji, I. D. and Fried, G. (2021) 'About Face: A Survey of Facial Recognition Evaluation'. Available at: https://arxiv.org/abs/2102.00813 (Accessed 26 March 2021).

2   The authors have published their research data in the form of an online spreadsheet available online at https://tinyurl.com/shbraqn.

portrait photographs and still video images. In 2007 the *Labeled Faces in the Wild* <16> (LFW) dataset led to Period III. This was the first dataset of faces sourced from the web and taken of individuals "in the wild" (i.e. in real life, as opposed to a staged photoshoot). Finally, the development of *DeepFace* <17> in 2014 – the first facial recognition model to beat human performance on a face verification task – brought us to the current period: Period IV. The DeepFace system, created by Facebook researchers, identified faces in digital images uploaded by users on the platform, and was trained with the now-dominant technique of deep learning.

Table 1: Historical Arcs of Facial Recognition Development

Period	Period I	Period II	Period III	Period IV
Years	before 1996	1996 – 2007	2007 – 2014	After 2014
Number of Datasets Created	5	37	33	45
Range of number of Images in a dataset (MIN-MAX)	56 – 14,126	120 – 121,589	154 – 750,000	642 – 50,000,000
Range of number of Subjects in a dataset (MIN-MAX)	4 – 1,199	10 – 37,437	32 – 40,395	50 – 14,400,000
Avarage number of images in a dataset	2,032	11,250	46,308	2,620,489
Avarage number of subjects in a dataset	136	1,641	4,078	75,726

Historical Arcs of Facial Recognition Development. It is clear that an increasing number of facial recognition image subjects and increasing dataset size occurred over time.

The significance of DeepFace in defining the current practices in facial recognition development cannot be overstated. The success of DeepFace at facial recognition led to an excitement for the widespread use of the resource-intensive technique of deep learning. This prompted a growing belief in the need for larger-scale datasets in order to satisfy the data requirements of such methods. As a result, datasets grew from including tens of thousands of images to incorporating millions from different sources (see for example, *MegaFace* <🔗18> and *VGG-Face2* <🔗19>). These mammoth datasets were at times optimized for *depth* (i.e. limiting the number of subjects but including many images for each subject, such as in VGG-Face2) and other times for *breadth* (i.e. containing many subjects but limiting images for each subject; see *MS-Celeb-1M* <🔗20> and MegaFace).

The new data requirements prompted a push to increase the size of datasets, and this fundamentally changed the way in which these datasets were sourced, curated and distributed. In Period I and II, face images were largely sourced from analogue image collections and photoshoots. In these cases, considerable attention was paid to issues of copyright and the protection of image ownership rights, as well as the informed consent of the individuals participating in the photoshoot. However, Labeled Faces in the Wild introduced a new inclination for the collection of images from the Web, where consent was difficult to acquire and images were unstaged and ultimately difficult to curate or properly account for. Whereas old datasets were typically digital images (of .png or .jpeg format) stored on physical hard drives, the digital images of online datasets are much more difficult to manage since their storage and distribution take shape in more varied, inconsistent forms.

See IMG 4 on page 179

Our survey also reveals that FPT tasks have been highly influenced by government and commercial interests providing either funding and/or establishing evaluation benchmarking competitions that shape the performance of facial processing technologies. For instance, the *NIST*

FRVT dataset in 2002 was funded by the Department of Homeland Security and contains data sourced from <ϟ21> "U.S. Department of State's Mexican non-immigrant Visa archive". The dominant use case for FPT has been – and still is – focused on access control, suspect identification, and video surveillance for the purpose of enhancing law enforcement capacity, and broadening surveillance for the purported benefit of public security. It is only recently that we have seen a greater proportion of industry participants as the developers of face image datasets. They are usually motivated by tasks and applications with broader commercial appeal, such as multiple classification tasks. In the past, many industry-developed datasets were kept private to protect user data. DeepFace, on the other hand, is a model developed by researchers at Facebook and trained on an internal face dataset sourced from content uploaded by the users of the platform. However, such projects are ultimately unreproducible, as other researchers cannot gain access to the protected data. It was only later, in Period IV, that we saw a rise in the development and release of publicly available face datasets developed by Microsoft, IBM and other corporate institutions.

Facial recognition technologies pose complex ethical and technical challenges. By virtue of being a biometric identifier, capturing an individual's face data inherently poses a privacy risk. As soon as the collection of face data became uncontrolled at scale – with data sourced from the Internet, and collected in such large quantities that it makes it difficult to track the image origins as well as the details of their curation and distribution – we witnessed a shift. Data development became cheap and accessible to anyone interested, rather than being an expensive process. Instead of being limited to constrained image settings, captured faces in recent datasets presented a larger number of subjects, covering a range of face poses and situations. However, this also led to a lack of caution for the consent of data subjects, and less control over the labels assigned to data, as well as the task design. The historical shifts in the development of face datasets have not been without consequence. Neglecting to unpack the complexity of these processes as well as to measure, analyse and articulate it to others is a disservice to the subjects who are most impacted by its careless deployment.

Dataset evaluation is a critical juncture in which we should provide transparency and even accountability over facial recognition systems – how they perform, what they're used for, and who they benefit. At a minimum, an important intervention moving forward is to standardise documentation practices; for example, of the model and the face datasets meant to be used in development or evaluation. Proposals such as Model Cards <🔗22> and Datasheets for Datasets <🔗23> – which aim to document and clarify the uses of the datasets and minimise their use in contexts that are not well suited – or the Data Privacy Label <🔗24> – that proposes a privacy label design drawing from nutrition, warning and energy labelling – can provide reporting guidelines to support the development of such practices as the new normal in the field. AI systems do not just enact harm when deployed; they can enact harm during their development and use. Producing datasets in a way that respects consent, privacy, and other democratic values helps us move closer to responsible machine learning development.

Hyperlinks

<𝒫1>   https://www.cnn.com/travel/
        article/airports-facial-
        recognition/index.html
<𝒫2>   https://www.reuters.com/investigates/
        special-report/usa-riteaid-software/
<𝒫3>   https://www.cnet.com/news/new-
        york-temporarily-bans-facial-
        recognition-in-schools/
<𝒫4>   https://www.perpetuallineup.org/
<𝒫5>   https://www.theguardian.com/
        law/2020/jul/22/exams-that-use-
        facial-recognition-are-fair-but-
        theyre-also-intrusive-and-biased
<𝒫6>   https://www.theguardian.
        com/cities/2019/may/29/
        new-york-facial-recognition-
        cameras-apartment-complex
<𝒫7>   https://medium.com/the-physics-
        arxiv-blog/the-face-recognition-
        algorithm-that-finally-
        outperforms-humans-2c567adbf7fc
<𝒫8>   https://www.nist.gov/news-events/
        news/2018/11/nist-evaluation-
        shows-advance-face-recognition-
        softwares-capabilities
<𝒫9>   https://www.independent.co.uk/
        news/uk/home-news/facial-
        recognition-london-inaccurate-
        met-police-trials-a8898946.html
<𝒫10>   https://news.sky.com/story/met-
        polices-facial-recognition-tech-

has-81-error-rate-independent-
report-says-11755941
<∂11> https://www.wsj.com/articles/
mtas-initial-foray-into-facial-
recognition-at-high-speed-
is-a-bust-11554642000
<∂12> https://www.nytimes.
com/2019/12/19/technology/
facial-recognition-bias.html
<∂13> https://www.wired.com/story/secret-
history-facial-recognition/
<∂14> http://www.historyofinformation.
com/detail.php?entryid=2495
<∂15> https://www.nist.gov/programs-
projects/face-recognition-
technology-feret
<∂16> http://vis-www.cs.umass.edu/lfw/
<∂17> https://en.wikipedia.
org/wiki/DeepFace
<∂18> http://megaface.cs.washington.edu/
<∂19> http://www.robots.ox.ac.
uk/~vgg/data/vgg_face2/
<∂20> https://www.microsoft.com/en-
us/research/project/ms-celeb-
1m-challenge-recognizing-one-
million-celebrities-real-world/
<∂21> https://www.nist.gov/publications/
face-recognition-vendor-test-
2002-evaluation-report
<∂22> https://arxiv.org/abs/1810.03993
<∂23> https://arxiv.org/abs/1803.09010
<∂24> https://cups.cs.cmu.edu/soups/2009/
proceedings/a4-kelley.pdf

Generative Representation
Heather Dewey-Hagborg

Artist Heather Dewey-Hagborg reflects about her work on the methodology of "forensic DNA phenotyping." In the essay, her work serves as a starting point to question the role of representation in a world of images based on computed models rather than an indexical link to reality.

For the past six years, I have been researching, writing and producing artworks engaging the methodology of "forensic DNA phenotyping." In brief, this is an emerging technology which attempts to depict a likeness of a person, to predict a person's physical features – namely their face – based on DNA alone. It is truly a method of the present technological moment, bringing together research in data science, machine learning, 3D scanning, 3D modelling and genomics to produce hybrid, predictive models. While the technology is not speculative <⛶1>, it is not accurate either.

Forensic DNA phenotyping has an air of infallibility to it because it is a form of DNA profiling technology, and this is easily conflated with DNA fingerprinting – the "gold standard" in police work. But phenotyping works differently. It is predictive, not identifying. It uses machine learning to make inferences about a person's traits based on their DNA, and like most machine learning models it has many problems with bias and stereotyping. This is particularly dangerous territory when working with genetics in the field of policing, a topic I have written about extensively elsewhere <&2>.

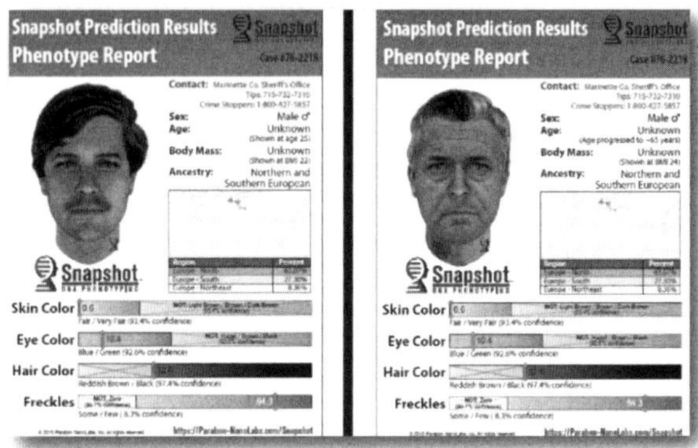

Marinette County investigation and DNA analysis by Parabon NanoLabs.

In this essay, I would like to explore a different aspect of this technology, one that has not been widely discussed, which might begin with the question: *is forensic DNA phenotyping a photographic process?* The question is significant because photography generally implies a subject that can be *represented*; it seems to have a certain claim on "reality." This is not an abstract or esoteric consideration, but one with real social and political consequences for how we see the world around us, and how we assess the truth claims of the images that circulate in our networks. It is of particular importance when considering the production of images used in police, state, and disciplinary contexts.

Generative representation is the production of images that appear "real", although they are constructed using completely artificial means. It describes the way in which an algorithmically produced image, like a portrait, might feel like an index to a real-world subject, even though it is entirely contrived. This phenomenon gives the generative image an authority that is essentially borrowed from the long history – and tremendous power – of representation in modernity.

Today, as we are engulfed by images of dubious origin propagated through politically structured networks, curated by opaque and sometimes discriminatory algorithms, it is an important moment to reflect on the power of the image, and its increasingly computational nature. In approaching this question, it is worth taking a minute to discuss how the phenotypic image is produced and to compare this with what we think of as "photography."

There are two primary forms of data that underpin the phenotypic model: genomic data, and 3D facial scans. We can intuit how these two datasets could be mined for correlations. For example, a data scientist might look for connections between the DNA code and the structure of the face that tend to co-occur; connections that don't necessarily imply causation, but simply appear together more often than we might expect. This is the fundamental insight that underpins the phenotypic impulse: the hard scientific problem of how genes actually create the proteins that make up human appearance doesn't have to be solved. Instead, it is "good enough" to make a prediction based on generalisations from piles of data, which can then be operationalised in contexts like policing.

The subject's DNA profile is fed into an algorithmic model of a face, which can be morphed along axes related to these correlations. Thus, behind the scenes, the code is essentially dragging a slider to make a face lighter or darker, more male or female, according to the parameters and limitations of the underlying model, and characterised by the data that determined the model in the first place.

Ultimately this results in a workflow in which genomic data is fed into software and a 3D face is generated as an output. Depending on the code of the software itself, we might also be able to generate many possible permutations of a person's face based on the structure of the data. For instance, I have used this process in my project *Probably Chelsea* where I algorithmically generated thirty different possible portraits of Chelsea Manning using an analysis of her DNA.

See IMG 5 on pages 180-181

If a trait is associated with different probabilistic phenotypes (as they generally are), then a set of possible faces might better show the potential of a person's DNA than a single image. The output of the phenotyping process might be a single face, or a slew of probable faces. There is no lens involved and there is no camera, but there is a production of a series of digital images.

Having unpacked DNA phenotyping, let's return to the question of whether phenotyping is a form of photography. In exploring this question, I will draw on Daniel Rubinstein's essay 'What is 21st Century Photography?'[1] commissioned by The Photographers' Gallery, and the series of lectures published on his website philosophyofphotography.net <℘3>.

---

[1]   Rubinstein, D. (2015) 'What is 21st Century Photography', *Viewpoints.* Available at: https://thephotographersgallery.org.uk/photography-culture/what-21st-century-photography.

Drawing on Jean-François Lyotard, Rubinstein suggests that the intellectual project of modernity was to represent the world, and we saw this unfold in technology, in political systems, in art, and in economics from the 14th century onward. Representation, he reminds us, was the task of painting until photography displaced it as a primary representational form. During a time of science, capitalism, and democracy, he argues: "representation was everywhere".

Rubinstein sees our contemporary moment as constituting a new technological and philosophical shift that calls representation itself into question. As daily life becomes increasingly abstracted, virtual, informatic and algorithmic, representation begins to lose its stability. We live in a world of images, but the character of those images has morphed into an "immersive economy". The image is a computational product; the outcome of an algorithmic process.

This shift demands a new approach to every field, including visual art and photography. An approach that utilises algorithmic methods to deconstruct our automated and virtualised society.

In Rubinstein's words:
"The problem is that in a post-Fordist society the locus of political agency and of cultural relevance has shifted from the object – as visually arresting as it might be – to the processes that (re)produce and distribute the object. Processes, however, by their own nature, are less visible and less representational than objects... In the 21st century, photography is not a stale sight for sore eyes, but the inquiry into what makes something an image. As such, photography is the most essential task of art in the current time."

This perspective paves the way for a slew of new imaging practices that are deeply computational. It opens the field of photography to non-lens-based generative processes, and it calls for an art form that exposes algorithmic production. The phenotypic image might seem to be an almost ideal candidate for this demand of contemporary photography. But it inevitably leads to a deeper question about the nature of representation itself.

If phenotyping can be held up as a prime example of new algorithmic, post-representational photographic practice, is phenotyping non-representational? Following this further brings us to another embedded question of whether a *model* is representational, as genomics and phenotyping, along with most of our algorithmic surroundings, are all generated by machine learning models. To analyse the representational power of generative images, we must first understand the model from which they are produced. To understand the true status of these pictures, we need to unpack their representational authority.

What is a model?

In a general sense, a model is a reduced description of a complex real-world system designed to fulfil a certain function. In machine learning, a model is an artifact produced through a training process in which a learning algorithm is exposed to data. The model is the outcome – the file or allocation of computer memory – that contains the structured result of a learning process.

For example, a model might be trained on input data that consist of images of fruit, tagged with the name of the variety of fruit. Once trained, the model will take any input image and assign it a category of fruit – regardless of whether the image has anything to do with fruit. Fruit determines the limits of the model's universe, and the specific fruits it was exposed to define its inductive bias.

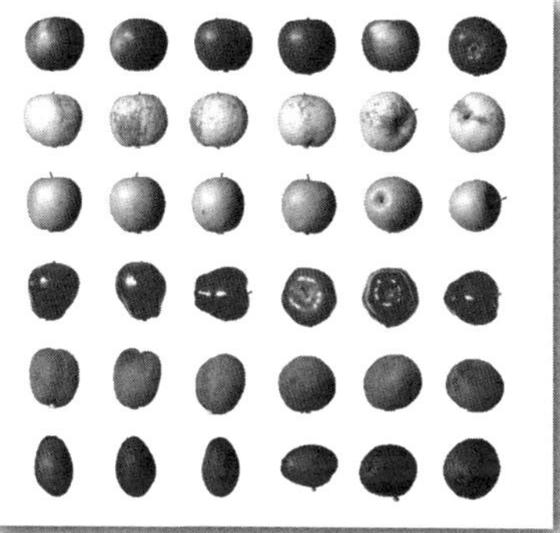

Fruit training dataset by Mihai Oltean and Horea Mureşan. Image License: MIT.

Does this model represent fruit?

We could see this model as representative, in the sense that sampling concrete images of fruit is the foundational basis of the model. Without a dataset of fruit experiences, there would be no model. However, to see this only as a representational system strikes me as too simplistic.

The model is constituted by a subject that is not singular but multiple. The model is always simultaneously all of the fruit it has ever seen, the statistical relations of this data, and the spaces in between actual data points. It is an attempt to capture an "essence" of what constitutes a specific category of fruit, such as *apple-ness*, to move beyond singular representation of the subject and into the realm of the abstract. It is important to recognise that such a form is always contingent and always limited. It is not, and should make no claim to be, a *universal* depiction of a fruit. It is precisely this leap from sampling and analysing data to the claim of essence from which so many problematics in machine learning derive. Nonetheless, the model contains the latent potential to concoct images of fruit that have never existed; in a sense *to imagine* fruit that goes beyond the simple exemplars of its experience.

The model, then, has some characteristics of representation but also transcends it. If a "sample" is representative of a homogenous set; if a politician is representative of their constituency; and if photography has the capacity to frame and "represent" a subject, a model appears to share this direct representational relationship while being structurally much more complex.

There is a danger in seeing models as simply a new form of representation because what they actually do – the way they function and act in society – is fundamentally different. The model shapeshifts. It can adopt a host of forms each of which may appear as certain, accurate, and as true as the last, but in reality, the model is a constellation; a fluid space of possibility.

The phenotypic image shows us the power of what we might then call *generative representation*: the production of an image that feels real, that feels like a direct representation, but is in actuality a phantom.

A single image produced through the DNA phenotyping process is always a lie. It feels compelling, it resonates with the viewer because it speaks to our representational history, but each singular image hides the incredible complexity and combinatorial potential that underlies it.

Returning to our initial question, it seems that forensic DNA phenotyping may indeed be a form of post-representational photography. Though it points to an area in which we should exercise caution; the phenotype borrows authority from the representational paradigm in a manner that might mask its intrinsically generative nature.

This brings us back to Rubinstein's call for an engaged 21st-century photography; one that is not backwards-looking but staring the future in the eyes with a critical gaze, using tools that interrogate algorithmic forms and aesthetics. Here the phenotype hovers before us, as a ghost from another era, exposing how easily we fall back into representational assumptions, and how sticky and complicated it might be to let go.

Hyperlinks

<⚓1>   https://snapshot.parabon-nanolabs.com
<⚓2>   https://thenewinquiry.com/sci-fi-crime-drama-with-a-strong-black-lead/
<⚓3>   http://philosophyofphotography.net

Unevenly Distributed
Florian Schmidt

Florian Schmidt, a researcher specialising in digital labour, has been following the value chain of German car companies backwards, trying to figure out who is doing the image labelling in the ambitious goal of producing fully autonomous vehicles. This text traces a geography of crowdsourced work and builds a detailed picture of the work conditions of the clickworkers producing datasets.

he Future Is Here! the title of Mimi Onuoha's video project[1] reflecting the human side of crowdsourced image labelling, is spot on. The stories I have been told by crowdworkers from across the globe doing this work full-time indeed often have an eerily Gibsonian ring to them, especially the stories from Venezuela. As a researcher specialising in digital labour, I had been following the value chain of German car companies backwards, trying to figure out who is doing the image labelling in the ambitious (and potentially over-ambitious) goal of producing fully autonomous vehicles.[2]

---

1   Schmidt refers here to the project *The Future is Here!* by Mimi Onuoha commissioned by The Photographers' Gallery as part of the Data/Set/Match programme. It was live on the gallery's Media Wall from 2nd of December 2019 until the 31st of January 2020. Schmidt's text was originally published on Unthinking Photography in March 2020, as a response to Onuoha's work.

2   This investigation was funded by the trade union related Hans Böckler Foundation and published as a report in German https://www.boeckler.de/fpdf/HBS-007110/p_study_hbs_417.pdf.

See IMG 6 and 7 on pages 182-183

As it turned out, the supposedly self-learning algorithms for the supposedly self-driving cars still need a myriad helping hands from humans to get things straight. And because the hype for AI in general, and for autonomous vehicles in particular, coincided with the collapse of the Venezuelan economy, people from this country made up to 75 per cent of the workforce on some of the largest platforms specialised on crowd-sourced image annotation in 2018 and 2019.

Typically, these images are stills taken from videos shot in traffic that are then manually annotated so that a machine can recognise each and every object within the frame. Humans have to, for example, draw so-called bounding boxes around cars or assign descriptive labels to every pixel in the video frame. These are called semantic segmentation maps and are currently the most common and most time-consuming of the various forms of image labelling.

The annotations have to be as detailed as possible so that the algorithm can learn to recognise objects, eventually without supervision, and learn to predict how these objects – vehicles or people – are going to behave in traffic. The reliability of the predictive machine-learning models is directly dependent on the precision of this "ground truth" or training data, and the production of this can only partly be automated.

A full semantic segmentation of an image can take a human up to two hours to complete, so for the automotive companies who need this data in bulk, fast and with high precision, this work can quickly get very expensive, especially if done in-house. This is why car companies use specialised outsourcing platforms such as Scale <🔗1>, Hive <🔗2>, Playment <🔗3>, Figure Eight <🔗4>, and, until recently, Mighty AI <🔗5>. Older platforms such as Amazon Mechanical Turk <🔗6>, which are also used for image annotation in other fields, are not precise enough for the demands of the car industry, which only buys data with a guaranteed accuracy of over 99%.

At Scale.com, the semantic segmentation of a single image with 99.2% accuracy costs the clients $6.40. They usually need hundreds of thousands of these images – this explains both why the industry is attracting a lot of capital and why it needs so many crowdworkers. In effect, the influx of capital is conjuring the crowd-based workforce into existence, rapidly creating an oversupply of labour needed to buffer the ebbs and flows in demand. The platforms translate the tasks into the language of the labour market they want to access, be it India, China or the Spanish speaking part of the world, and the workers find their way to the tasks on offer, for example, through special forums on Reddit <🔗7>. For the car AI tasks, hardly any cultural knowledge is needed, just the ability to focus for long hours.

In contrast to content moderators working for US social media platforms, who, as a legacy of colonialism, are often based in the Philippines,[3] the workers doing image annotation for the car industry don't suffer from the type of work as such. It is exhausting work, but not soul-crushing, and it can give workers a rewarding sense of mastery to finish an image with

---

3   See for example the book by Sara T. Roberts *Behind the Screen* (published by Yale University Press) or the 2018 documentary *The Cleaners* by Hans Block and Moritz Riesewieck.

high accuracy. The workers do, however, suffer from the extreme precariousness of the work – the constant worry whether an algorithm or management will allow them to work the next day. On a good week, on a good platform, they can make $50; in a bad week only $10, which is still more than what they can earn offline with a regular job in Venezuela.

At first glance, the people training the AI systems are normal knowledge workers, sitting at their laptop, clicking away at the Internet all day like most free-lancers. Their home-office, as Mimi Onuoha's project shows, might look similar to yours. Yet, to make ends meet, they not only have to subjugate themselves to algorithmic management and gamification regiments but also, more importantly, they have to navigate highly complex, volatile and opaque global markets for the production of ground truth data.

They work as freelance sub-sub-contractors, switching back and forth between different platforms that funnel the work from supranational corporations to people in the Global South, while the car companies try their best to stay anonymous.

"We don't know who we are actually working for", says Jose, a 26-year-old civil engineer from Venezuela, "but we would feel better, more part of the project, if we did. We used to see quite a lot of images from Germany, we assumed from Volkswagen and Porsche, but not anymore; recently it was more California, San Diego, that's why we thought of Tesla."

Ironically, the sub-sub-outsourcing goes so far that the car companies and crowdsourcing platforms also can't be sure who is actually doing the work, because the workers in turn are renting out their accounts to others when they are not using them. Both ends of the tenuous sub-outsourcing chain are unknown to each other.

While the Venezuelan workers are hyper-connected via international groups on Slack and Discord – official channels by the companies and unofficial private channels to help each other with the tasks and rent out accounts – they are often physically stuck in abject poverty with out-dated computing equipment. Their livelihood is constantly threatened by blackouts, corruption, organised crime, and food-shortages on one side of the screen, and the capriciousness of algorithmic management, venture capital flows and geopolitical sanctions on the other.

Douglas, a 21-year-old engineering student from Venezuela, explained to me via Skype:

"The situation is better than five years ago, mainly because – this may sound crazy to you – most of the criminals have fled the country. The crime rate is still really high, but it is more secure now to go outside without getting robbed. But there is not much for me out there anyway, because I do almost everything here on the computer."

However, staying at home didn't protect Douglas from getting robbed:

"During one of the blackouts, people climbed into my courtyard, where, right under my window I keep some livestock for extra food. They took a few chickens and climbed back. Behind my house, there is a kind of wasteland with improvised settlements and from there people must have observed that I have chickens here."

Douglas and Jose both used to work for the Seattle-based Spare5 <🔗🔒>, by far the most popular of about a dozen crowdsourcing platforms specialised on data annotation for the automotive industry. Until recently, the company was known to its corporate clients as Mighty AI. It has become a common phenomenon that these crowdsourcing firms appear Janus-faced with complementary brand names and websites: they have a customer-facing front, emphasising their AI prowess, and a worker-facing back-entrance emphasising the opportunity to quickly earn a handful of dollars. (Scale AI is actually remotasks <⚭9>; The Hive AI is actually Hive Work <⚭10>.)

In the summer of 2019 Uber ATG acquired Mighty AI, discontinued that side of the brand and began restructuring how work is organised on the accompanying worker platform Spare5, which at that time had a freelance workforce of half a million people. Three quarters of these so-called "Fives" came from Venezuela. Immediately after the acquisition and without notice or proper explanation, Uber geo-blocked all Venezuelan workers from accessing the platform. Andrea, a long-time member of the "Super5s", an elite group of a few hundred of the most productive and accurate workers, hitherto always in close contact with management, recalls:

"When we realised that us losing access was not a technical error, but an intentional action to leave us on the sidelines for an indefinite time, it was as if the floor under our feet disappeared."

At first it seemed that Uber's exclusion of Venezuelan workers was due to US sanctions against President Nicolás Maduro, because the workers got paid only three weeks later and only after signing a statement that they are not affiliated with the Government.

One of the few viable alternatives for Venezuelan online workers is to grind for virtual gold or dragon bones in the old school online role-play game *RuneScape* <∞11>, or to level up characters in *League of Legends* <∞12>. A type of labour done for clients in the Global North, who prefer to outsource the drudgery of their hobby to skip a few rungs of the ladder in their make-believe status game. All sides in this situation make an arbitrage from an extremely uneven distribution of wealth, time and power in a hyper-connected global market for information and labour. Since the beginning of 2020, Venezuelan workers are allowed back in at Spare5, while other countries are now shut out without explanation. At the time of writing (February 2020) web-traffic to Spare5 is 67% from Venezuela again.

The crowdsourced production of ground truth image data is likely to grow even further over the coming years. Yet, from the workers' perspective, it remains an inherently unsustainable and unpredictable line of work that is threatened at every point by additional layers of automation and sub-outsourcing. Machines will be able to do more and more of the image annotation tasks, but will have to be continuously trained by humans for new tasks and new edge cases. Paradoxically, while it is hard to automate the training of the machines, it is easy to automate the training of the people who are then going to train the machines.

Within these systems, the crowdworkers are just another cognitive processing layer within a much larger automation and outsourcing apparatus. Humans and machines form a cybernetic organism, built from layers of artificial and human intelligence. Interestingly, new specialist platforms try to get a competitive advantage over each other by experimenting with different stacking-orders – alternating successions of humans and algorithms. In doing this, the platforms resemble not only what Benjamin Bratton has described as "The Stack",[4] but there is also a structural self-similarity reminiscent of the various hidden processing layers within the neural networks.

Because of the complexity, opacity, and contingency of these global image-processing stacks, only raw input and annotated output can be observed – what happens in between remains practically unknowable. It is important to keep in mind that all the major car companies train their neural networks based on different, and differently produced, data sets, with varying human-machine layers and varying classes of objects involved. If we get a future with fully autonomous vehicles, different car brands might show varyingly erratic behaviour in edge cases, depending on the diet of images they have been fed. Authorities responsible for traffic safety would either have to make extensive behaviourist tests with the cars, of course without ever being able to check all edge cases; demand a fully transparent and standardised image annotation and training process from all brands, or even only allow one standardised universal system that all brands contribute to. Most likely, however, they will only allow these vehicles in controlled special zones, in which all edge cases caused by humans or animals can be excluded. For now, the future struggles with a present reality that is far messier than can be accounted for.

---

4   Bratton, B.H. (2016) *The Stack: On Software and Sovereignty*, Cambridge, MA and London: The MIT Press.

Hyperlinks

<🔗1> https://scale.com/

<🔗2> https://thehive.ai/

<🔗3> https://www.telusinternation-
al.com/solutions/ai-data-solu-
tions?INTCMP=ti_playment

<🔗4> https://appen.com/

<🔗5> https://www.geekwire.com/2019/uber-
acquires-seattle-startup-mighty-
ai-fuel-push-self-driving-cars/

<🔗6> https://www.mturk.com/

<🔗7> https://www.reddit.com/r/beermoney/

<🔗8> https://gt-test1.auth.us-east-1.
amazoncognito.com/login?client_
id=3vgcc8j5oukc11up0u1k78ks6u&redi-
rect_uri=https%3A%2F%2Fapp.spare5.
com%2Foauth2%2Fidpresponse&re-
sponse_type=code&scope=email%20
openid&state=6Kymmh2m5MaWaJEECo%2B-
sK%2F7%2BUFh30kJ%2B0jzxNYs7CdYRGs6k1d-
BWA6FLW7jWSm9m7fSr2%2B0aq571EZxDx-
uo081j9FHX%2FUCYvkjiI1TF4isX4uPF-
GaH2qHb%2FGxU1s3XoR1UkqCrdyGYdDfE-
6JYkSC9q6bZYFe18%2FvkvprwD04ERxP-
Dr18jKT1skYjY%2FWIoV9%2F5Ihomic0

<🔗9> https://www.remotasks.com/

<🔗10> https://hivemicro.com/

<🔗11> https://www.gamebyte.com/pow-
er-outage-in-venezuela-causes-eco-
nomic-crisis-in-runescape/

<🔗12> https://play.eune.league-
oflegends.com/en_PL

Decision Space:
Nicolas Malevé in conversation with Sebastian Schmieg

For a period of about four months in 2016-2017, the images displayed on the pages of The Photographers' Gallery's website were overlaid with four intriguing keywords: *problem*, *solution*, *past* and *future*. At the same time, on the Media Wall of the gallery, a script recursively exploiting Google's "recursive image search" produced a continuous chain of images. These two works by the artist Sebastian Schmieg critically explored the impact of machine learning on visual culture, as well as the imbalances and asymmetries in the production of artificial intelligence. The following is an excerpt from a conversation between the artist and Nicolas Malevé in 2017 that focuses on the project *Decision Space*, and the processes and politics of image annotation.

Nicolas Malevé: Shall we make a start by talking a bit about your background? It is interesting to sketch not just how you came to do what you are doing today, but also how it fits in the context of The Photographers' Gallery digital programme.

Sebastian Schmieg: Well, like many people, I started dabbling with the Internet. I was lucky that we had an early Internet connection so I started making websites. I initially aspired to become a web designer but I ended up studying with the net artist Olia Lialina. Back then I didn't realise how much this influenced me.

I first did some studies in computer science, which was interesting, but I was totally missing the creative part. I continued studying at the University of the Arts in Berlin and I always had a strong focus on programming. I wouldn't say that this element could be found in all my projects, but it's a mindset that I have. That background for me connects to the *Decision Space* project.[1] Studying in the design department, I was asked to create solutions, which I reluctantly did, but I was always better at looking into problems. [Laughter]

NM So you found yourself some good problems to show and discuss?

SS Yeah, I did. And that's a process that has stuck with me.

NM Would you like to describe your project *Decision Space* commissioned by The Photographers' Gallery?

SS There are two strong currents running through my practice. One, which started with *Search by Image*,[2] is looking at computer vision and archives of images. The other one is looking at how this constant connectivity changes the way we work.

1   *Decision Space* (2016) was an online commission by Sebastian Schmieg that examined how machine vision datasets are created. Developed on the The Photographers' Gallery website, the commission invited visitors to assign all the images available on the website to one of four categories: Future, Past, Problem and Solution. You can find out more about the project here: with https://thephotographersgallery.org.uk/whats-on/decision-space.

2   *Search by Image* (2011-ongoing) is a series of algorithmic videos by Sebastian Schmieg that explore Google's image search processes. In 2016 a version of this work, under the title *Search by Image, Live (Lena/Fabio)* was presented at The Photographers' Gallery Media Wall. In this live version of the work, Schmieg used Google's reverse image search engine to unpack the growing narratives around the infamous image of Lena Forsén previously Söderberg. You can find out more about the project here: https://thephotographersgallery.org.uk/whats-on/sebastian-schmieg-search-image-live-lenafabio.

These two things together brought me to look into neural networks and how they learn to look at an image and how they understand it. I realised that at the core of artificial intelligence there is a huge amount of people who are tagging or describing images for very little money, and on the other hand people like you and me – that everything we do is also captured into these datasets to train artificial intelligence.

I got interested in what these systems are trained on because, given the extent to which they are used and will be used – from smartphones to surveillance to warfare, the photographic training data sets have serious ethical implications that need to be addressed. So when somebody is sitting there doing a job for really shitty money that influences the outcome of the system too.

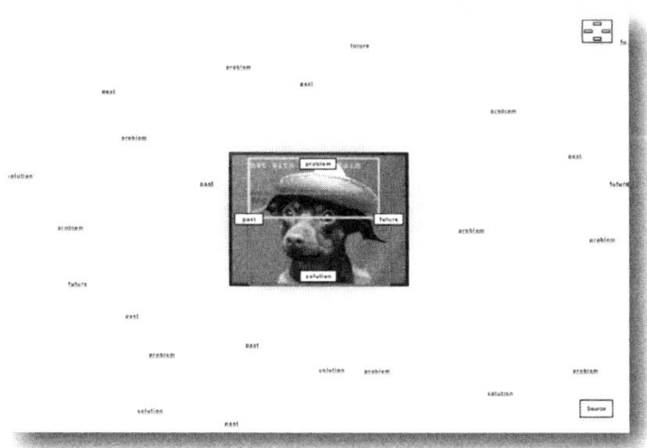

Screenshot from the *Decision Space* interface
(2016-2017) © Sebastian Schmieg

Decision Space is an attempt to create a new dataset, which you can then use to train a so-called artificial intelligence or a neural network. I created that dataset by using all the photos that were part of The Photographers' Gallery online image collection. Visitors to the website could then help categorise each image according to four choices: problem, solution, past, future. So, for instance, when you would go to the gallery's website you could decide for each image by saying "that for me represents the problem, the solution, the past or the future".

See IMG 10 on page 185

At the same time, there is also a dedicated website for *Decision Space*[3] that shows all images from the online collection, in a sequence, one after another. The website also recreates an interface similar to the one you use as a dedicated image annotator or classifier, as a Mechanical Turk worker[4] – so to speak.

NM In your work, you often reverse-engineer either an existing algorithm or how people are annotating datasets. But now you take the decision, and the responsibility, to constitute the dataset yourself. As this is the first decision to make, I wondered

---

3   An archived version of the original website is available here: http://deci-sion-space.com/.

4   According to Amazon's website "Amazon Mechanical Turk (MTurk) is a marketplace for completion of virtual tasks that requires human intelligence. The Mechanical Turk service gives businesses access to a diverse, on-demand, scalable workforce and gives Workers a selection of thousands of tasks to complete whenever it's convenient". Find out more on: https://www.mturk.com/worker/help.

what kind of questions it brings and how it is different from your previous works?

SS I wanted to create the situation of a Mechanical Turk – which we all are of course: *select all images, tag your friend, rate this product* – rather than using the actual Mechanical Turk. I was interested in how I could set up this whole little factory myself and understand how this assembly line works. For example, datasets are often based on photos from Flickr. There, people often upload their photos using a Creative Commons license, since of course "sharing is caring". But this sharing also means that their photos might end up being used by Microsoft or other companies to train their systems.

Looking at The Photographers' Gallery website, I was trying to find a way to speak about appropriating the work of all these photographers, and the cognitive resources of all visitors to the website.

NM Most of the time, in the case of Mechanical Turk workers, there are a lot of precautions that are set in advance in order to not ambiguously label images. So for instance when Fei-Fei Li explains[5] how they made ImageNet, she shows how every time the annotator needs to annotate an image, the annotator is tested: "Do you understand the meaning of the label?"

It is only when the worker has passed the test that (s)he can begin the annotation. Which leads me to your decision to stay ambiguous. The four words "past", "present", "problem", "solution"

5   See for example this Ted Talk from March 2015 where Fei-Fei Li explains 'How we're teaching computers to understand images': https://www.ted.com/talks/fei_fei_li_how_we_re_teaching_computers_to_understand_pictures.

appear without definition or context. It is puzzling and enigmatic for the visitors of the website as they don't know what they are supposed to put behind those words. But that's also a decision you made – I was wondering how you came to that decision?

SS The stage that we currently are with AI technologies is still a naive one. I wanted to extrapolate what is at stake in the future and suggest that there are some concepts, in the context of AI, that are neither true nor false and not as innocent as dogs or cats. The projects play with the idea that in the process of annotating there might be concepts towards which the workers can be biased because of their background; their cultural background for example. Obviously there is no exact future, or problem, so for me, the dataset shows how being totally contradictory can still make sense.

You can look at an image and say "I can understand why a person clicked on 'future' but I also understand why another person clicked on 'past'." I really wanted to explore this ambiguity and in a way break the logic of "you just need to scale up these systems" in order to construct this super-intelligent thing. I think ambiguity and scaling do not go well together.

In terms of my influences when creating this work, I was really fascinated by the MIT moral machine as absolutely problematic as well as revealing, especially considering that it is an approach that determines what a car should do in a situation of dilemma.

NM   Could you say a few words about your work *Seg-mentation.Network*?[6] Because I tend to read these projects side by side, as two different approaches to the same problem.

SS   Yes, exactly.

To explain it briefly, *Segmentation.Network* is looking at the Microsoft COCO dataset, which is quite a special one because it's not only saying "okay in this photo there is a dog and the owner, and the dog is there." Instead, the data has proper segmentation. For example, there are lines around the dog and the owner, locating them and tracing their shapes, so the boundaries of the objects in the photo are clearly delineated, which makes the data less opaque. And these data have been created by Mechanical Turks, click by click.

I was then trying to highlight two things: first, the amount of labour that goes into these processes. Most of the time when you hear about these systems, it's either about clever engineers, or about the super-intelligent algorithm, but it's hardly ever about the people that are working at the core of it. Secondly, I wanted to look at how this assembly line defines computer vision: the machine can only see what is inside a segment. Everything that is outside of this will remain unrecognised or deemed irrelevant. For me, a key point in both these projects is to realise that it is not just these people doing the work

6   *Segmentation.Network* (2016) is an online project by Sebastian Schmieg that plays back over 600,000 segmentations manually created by crowd workers for Microsoft's COCO image recognition dataset. This dataset is based on photos from Flickr and is used in machine learning for training and testing. Find out more here: http://sebastianschmieg.com/segmentation-network/.

but it is actually all of us. So, with *Decision Space* I wanted to highlight that we are the same, we are also workers, cloud-workers, turning our cultural background and our biases into data and software.

NM There is a dimension of "reverse engineering" in your work that is very strong – in *Search by Image*, for example, you probe the search algorithm in order to understand how it works. I'm intrigued by this practice as the more I read about machine learning algorithms, the more I notice computer scientists are quite puzzled by the behaviour of their algorithmic creations. They cannot understand what's happening by simply looking at the code.

Technologists have now developed a method called "adversarial imaging", where they feed images instead of code into a program to understand how it works. I was thinking about how you uploaded a transparent image to Google in a version of *Search by Image*; I wondered if this was already a form of "adversarial imaging"? Perhaps there is now the scope for the computer sciences to fully embrace the importance of visual practices of computing not just as a hobby, but as core to their discipline.

SS Absolutely. I recently started reading *The Human Condition* by Hannah Arendt, a book from the 1950s, which I find relevant in this discussion. In the prologue of the book, Arendt explains that we have come to a point where humans have the logic and the math to create machines and can prove that the math works. However, what we lack is the precise language to describe what the machine is and what it does. And even though it's our own creation, we might not understand it any more.

Today we find ourselves needing machines to do our thinking, seeing and speaking. So we get into the position where we have to follow our own creations. Or, as Arendt says, we have: "indeed become the helpless slaves, not so much of our machines as of our know-how, thoughtless creatures at the mercy of every gadget which is technically possible, no matter how murderous it is."[7]

Perhaps, then, the role of visual practice is to help grasp what we don't understand anymore.

With respect to your point about reverse engineering, initially I would have said OK, *Search by Image* utilises this as a strategy, to some degree. But then you would need to reverse engineer my project to understand how I used Google Search, so it's messy. Perhaps a better question is: "what would I find if I reverse engineered Google Image Search – would I find a system that could be used in a way that I might find more interesting?"

I wonder whether such an example of reverse engineering could liberate something that has the potential to be used differently. Or perhaps the process itself would reveal a power that we wouldn't want to use any further?

NM That brings me, maybe, to the last question. I'm interested in the connections between users and workers in this process: the user who exchanges images on social media, and the outsourced worker who annotates images on Amazon Mechanical Turk. What kind of connections can we make between

---

7   Arendt, H. (2019) *The Human Condition*, Chicago: University of Chicago Press. Second Edition. p. 3.

somebody who is working all day, describing and processing images, trying to make as much money as they can… and people updating and annotating their Facebook or Flickr accounts? I can see that there are clicks produced by both groups, but are these two contexts so different? For instance, with Google, when do they need professional image annotators, and when do they need data generated by internet users "in the wild"?

SS First of all, I think the connection between a person uploading a picture, and then another person – who is absolutely not the intended audience – looking at that picture and annotating it is an interesting one. There is this really weird connection between the image annotator to other people who are actually living their lives, sharing nice photographic moments on their online accounts.

When you speculate how many professionals Google requires, I'm beginning to think that Google doesn't actually need any professionals. For instance, for the past five years, Silvio Lorusso and I have been collecting all CAPTCHAs that we solved,[8] and I think I have a good understanding of how these systems evolve and how they put the user to work.

Interestingly, the latest reCAPTCHAs that we recorded ask users to draw a line around street signs – not like a rectangle, but a proper line, like in a Segmentation Network. This is what you or I do when

8   Schmieg refers here to the work *Five Years of Captured Captchas* (2017) that he created with Silvio Lorusso. The work is a series of five leporello books that span a total length of 90 meters, chronicling every single captcha that the artists have solved over the course of five years.

we have to convince Google that we are not a robot. So apparently for them, it's work that anybody can do. They just need to generate enough data.

NM So can we compare our clicks to those who actually make a living, or try to make a living, through Mechanical Turk?

SS That's why I was so puzzled by the conversation with the worker in Sri Lanka with whom I collaborated as part of the project *How to appear offline forever* (2015)[9] – she was so happy with the outsourcing platform, while I thought it was terrible.

The employer who hires somebody on Mechanical Turk can view the Turkers' screen anytime, to make sure they actually work. My collaborator really thought this surveillance was justified in the name of quality because she believed other people don't work, but act as if they do. I find this really messy, but what I'm always trying to do is to make a connection. It is not just "them", it is all of us, and the system itself, which is exploitative. Artificial Intelligence is built on an exploitative system and it is dehumanising as well; it dehumanises the workers as well as the rest of us. I really

---

9　As part of the project *How to appear offline forever* (2015), a piece about visibility, labour and colonialism in a networked world, Schmieg worked with two writers in Sri Lanka. As he mentioned in the full interview [part II, available on Unthinking Photography] the only way for him to work with them was to use an outsourcing platform. As he points out: "...Later I got the opportunity to travel to Sri Lanka, and talk about the work at the Colomboscope. I invited one of the two ladies I worked with, and had a conversation with her. It was very important for me to involve her perspective on it and to make clear that this is a shared project. It is easy to talk about bad working conditions and so on, but it is very different to hear about it from people who are actually subject to it, but who still think the platform is great."

hope movements like platform cooperativism have a future where we could all together – workers and users – own the platforms and the infrastructure in general. After all, we're the ones building and maintaining it.

NM So you think that, with fairer conditions, this kind of AI "training" method which requires millions of clickworkers could be interesting or…?

SS That's what I was trying to get at with your question about reverse engineering. At its core, is such a system already exploitative by design or not? I was recently asked in a talk whether I think neural networks are exploitative. My response was, "No, it's just an algorithm." On reflection, I still think this is true, but the whole setup is problematic and I don't see how it could become a positive thing any time soon.

NM I'm struggling with that myself. I've been doing some reading exploring where the method of "training" used in neural networks comes from. It is linked to a certain practice in psychology of testing animal intelligence, where lab animals were either rewarded or punished. It seems that this historical background cannot be taken lightly, because when you see how "training" is implemented via platforms such as Mechanical Turk, the history of training in the lab comes to mind. The Turkers are not just doing their work; they are opening up their cognitive processes to scrutiny. They have to respond to challenges very fast and are rewarded by the requester, or not, with no further obligation on the requester's part to explain why he accepts or refuses to pay for the work done. Just as the lab animal needs to find its way through the maze, the Turker needs to figure out what triggers the reward or the punishment. To consider which answer to give in order to avoid the requester's rejection without any possibility of establishing contact or negotiation. In the case of an image description task for example, what is an appropriate label? Which one corresponds to the requester's expectation?

Behind every choice of words, there is the possibility of gaining or losing the task's reward. And in turn, the algorithm is implemented with similar methods. The more the algorithm approximates the rules that are in the training data, the more it is rewarded and the more the processes that lead to this successful approximation are reinforced in the programme. If the learning in machine learning is reduced to reward and punishment, what kind of intelligence is produced there? It's true that it is really important to pay the Turkers better. But is it enough to really change what is wrong with the system? Where should we look for a more fruitful approach to training and learning?

SS I think the connection to training an animal, or to making these experiments, is spot on. I'm also thinking of the time-motion study technique, which is a method to determine the most efficient movement of an industrial worker, so it can be extrapolated to all workers in the name of optimisation and efficiency. And in the case of machine vision, as we've been discussing, the task is to extract little bits of knowledge, bit by bit… So, on the one hand, there is the training of the system, but on the other hand the misery of the continuous draining of cognitive resources. You suck it out bit by bit, and this doesn't change even when you pay better. Ultimately, it is about what stuff you can extract, until, in the end, you don't need the person any more – like in Kurt Vonnegut's *Player Piano*.

This was my point in generating photos based on *This is the Problem, the Solution, the Past and The Future* dataset for my online commission at The Photographers' Gallery. Of course, these images won't represent the future 100%, but I'm also – in a very unsuccessful way – saying, "Look! I've got all your photographers on my computer now, I can make my own photos through your previous work...!"

Recovering Lost Narratives in Epic Kitchens

xtine burrough and Sabrina Starnaman

This article is an overview of the projects *Epic Hand-washing in a Time of Lost Narratives* and *A Kitchen of One's Own* that were presented at The Photographers' Gallery during the first lockdown of the Covid-19 pandemic. In this text the artists make technical and conceptual links between the two projects and discuss their practice of working with datasets, creating speculative remixes from them, and making sense of life during a pandemic.

Created for online viewers during the Covid-19 lockdown, *Epic Hand Washing in a Time of Lost Narratives* <∞1> is an iteration of the installation *A Kitchen of One's Own,* a project commissioned for The Photographers' Gallery Media Wall as part of the Data/Set/Match programme.[1] Both projects juxta-

---

1   In March 2020, we were ready to ship our project, *A Kitchen of One's Own,* to The Photographers' Gallery in London for display on the 2.7 by 3 metre Media Wall. As one of three commissions for the gallery's series Data/Set/Match, a year-long programme seeking new ways to present, visualise and interrogate contemporary image datasets, *A Kitchen of One's Own* confronts a large, open-source video dataset of people in their kitchens. This 2018 dataset generated by the Epic Kitchens research group became the visual base upon which we juxtaposed narratives centering on women in the kitchen.

pose the *Epic Kitchens* dataset with a textual dataset of our own creation to reveal the arbitrary nature of information preservation and highlight the constructed nature of digitised materials. Blurring the lines between art and archive, or information and dataset, these projects further argue on the digital dataset as an authority of knowledge curation. These projects act as an entry point to reflect upon the meaning, and cost, of being in the kitchen in social isolation (*Epic Hand Washing in a Time of Lost Narratives*), and as a woman (*A Kitchen of One's Own*). This text is an overview of both projects, weaving a thread between the technical and the conceptual: the projects are linked historically by the writing and arguments put forth by Virginia Woolf, technologically by computational juxtapositions of text and image, as well as poetically in the viewer's experience through a speculative remix.

These speculative remix projects are an intervention in Epic Kitchens <∞2>, the largest dataset of first person vision filmed with head-mounted cameras.[2] <∞3> The computer scientists working on this project are training machine learning to "advance first-person vision, enabling improvements in robotics, healthcare and augmented reality."[3] Researchers assign to each video verbs like "wash", "peel", "put", or "rub" in order to describe and categorise events. The Epic Kitchen re-

---

2   The 2018 set was created in 32 participant kitchens across four cities, and culminated in 55 hours of footage shot at 60 frames per second, that is, more than 11 million frames of footage. Videos in the dataset are annotated using live audio commentary and tagged by Epic Kitchens researchers with 125 verb classes and 331 noun classes.

3   University of Bristol (2018, April 19) Largest-ever computer vision dataset from wearable cameras. Available at: https://www.bristol.ac.uk/news/2018/april/epic-kitchens.html (Accessed 12 May 2020).

search team made available a set of 268 videos to train machine learning with segments tagged with pairs of nouns and verbs. For our projects, we re-exported and reused the training videos in the Epic Kitchens' 2018 set; we, therefore, present a parallel set of literary texts in poetic dialogue with the original verbs or noun/verb pairings that appear at keyframes in these everyday kitchen recordings.

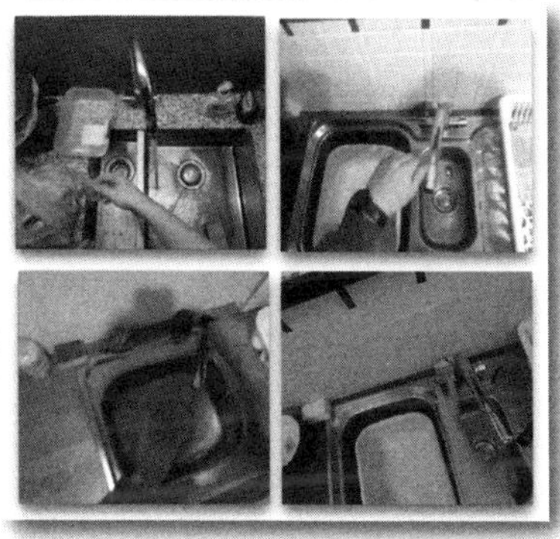

Still frames from four videos in the Epic Kitchens training set tagged with the verb "wash" and the noun "hand."

<u>From A Kitchen of One's Own</u>
<u>to Epic Hand Washing in</u>
<u>a Time of Lost Narratives</u>

In 1929, Virginia Woolf gave voice to many women's experiences of living in a patriarchy with the book *A Room of One's Own*. Woolf's essay was the conceptual beginning for our first project *A Kitchen of One's Own*, which subsequently asks: What does it mean to be a woman in a kitchen or for a woman to have power over the food she makes? When the Covid-19 pandemic postponed the installation of *A Kitchen of One's Own*, it got us thinking about literature that had been written about being in quarantine, being sick, as well as living amid a pandemic. In 1926, Woolf wrote the lesser-known extended essay, 'On Being Ill' <∞4> about the 1918 influenza pandemic. In this essay Woolf probes how the English language is incapable of expressing the lived reality of severe illness. The intensity of high fever, delirium, and aches is not something we can accurately convey using the expressive means at our disposal. According to Woolf, such a situation needs a new language, and one that relies heavily on figurative language and images. The COVID-19 pandemic is a novel experience for us, but not a novel experience in the course of human history; we have the insight of the past to draw from in order to give voice to our own experience and to lend a narrative that may explain what we are enduring.

Our project *Epic Hand Washing in a Time of Lost Narratives*, therefore, juxtaposes the mundane experience of living in quarantine with expressions that sought to capture the reality of human experience – a reality that writers like Woolf and Camus thought could only be expressed with poetic or figurative language <∞5>.

See IMG 8 on page 184

Moreover, when we experience a once-in-a-lifetime global event, humanity loses its established meaning-making narratives. As we look backward on events, emotions, and the loss of the familiar, we need to construct new stories while assembling a new existence. How do historical narratives and the mundane work of surviving day-to-day in isolation play out in our lived experience? What appears as an everyday activity in the original Epic Kitchens videos, in our work becomes charged with intimate human narratives, which have been created by writers across time to understand life within pandemics.

See IMG 9 on page 184

Texts written during pandemics, or reflecting back on life during that time, offered valuable insights into our contemporary experience as the Covid-19 pandemic was unfolding. Since we had been working with the Epic Kitchens dataset just prior to the Covid-19 pandemic, we were intimately familiar with the first-person kitchen videos. As our quarantine began, we were especially mindful of our own experiences in the kitchen. This was a moment for us in which life did more than imitate our art – our lives were like a performance of the art we were making. As we were peeling, cutting, washing, and so on, we, too, were making sense of life during a pandemic. Thus, we turned to novels, plays, poetry, and essays written during or about life during pandemics from the bubonic plague to the global influenza pandemic of 1918-19. Our selection of texts includes authors such as William Shakespeare, Virginia Woolf, Albert Camus, Katherine Anne Porter, William Maxwell, and Giovanni Boccacio, who experienced outbreaks of yersinia pestis (bubonic plague) and the H1N1 influenza outbreak of 1918-19. These texts address the horror of being sick, the fear of becoming infected, the grief of loss, as well as the mundane life of quarantine. While reading or rereading these works, we looked for quotes that (1) spoke to the experiences we were having or witnessing around the globe, and (2) were short enough to be viewed in juxtaposition with video in an average web browser.

The quotes were then juxtaposed with the selected videos from Epic Kitchens to create new narratives not just about kitchens but also about our contemporary experience of domestic spaces. Tagged with the noun "hand" and the verb "wash", our poetic browser-based project *Epic Hand Washing in a Time of Lost Narratives* centers 68 unique video clips redacted from the much longer videos in the Epic Kitchens dataset. Each new clip is thirty seconds long, and a randomly-selected quote from the set of literary texts is juxtaposed over the clips as they are displayed online, creating a series of unique pairings for the viewer. This provocative overlay invites the reader to create their own story about what is happening in the displayed kitchen, and to reflect on happenings in their own kitchen during the pandemic. If a viewer holds their cursor over the text, they will see the title of the book, play, or essay to which it is attributed. Clicking on the text leads to a new video and quote juxtaposition that advances the narrative and creates new correlations.[4] This methodology of associating images with text and creating new

---

4   This project is published in a Creative Commons license (Zero v1.0 Universal) on Github and the videos were first streaming from the Vimeo collection, Epic Hand Washing – a sub dataset of videos from 'Epic Kitchens' that have been transformed in size and duration, and re-exported and compressed for streaming online. The site was remade to stream from The Photographers' Gallery server as Vimeo's streaming was notably slower in the UK than in the US. The navigation at the bottom of the project links to these collections and to a spreadsheet that shows the complete bibliography for the project. A form in which viewers can suggest additional quotes is also linked from the bottom navigation tool.

narratives is central in our work and a framework that we also used in the creation of the original project for the Media Wall.

A Kitchen of One's Own

The kitchen is a complex space for women: it can be a realm of creativity and nurturing, a place of domestic oppression, a sphere of professional success, or a work environment rife with sexual harassment. In A Kitchen of One's Own we curated textual selections in English that explore this multitude of experiences across cultures and foodways,[5] while also being in conversation with the everyday scenes of making food in domestic kitchens from around the world. From women writers to women artists, the kitchen is a space that holds possibility for reinterpretation.

Many women move between the spaces of the domestic kitchen and the professional one, but their presence is regarded differently in different spaces. In a 2016 interview for *Another Gaze Journal*,[6] Martha Rossler said, "Women are always teetering on the brink in the liminal space between the public and the private, and societies have very strict rules about women and their appearance in public. Whereas it is taken for granted that women ... own the domestic sphere ...". In our work, we call attention to those tensions between pri-

---

5   Originating from social science, "foodways" describes not just the production and consumption of food, but also the intersections of food with culture and history.

6   Another Gaze Journal (2016, February 24) *In Conversation with Martha Rosler (Interview)* [Video], YouTube. Available at: https://www.youtube.com/watch?v=EMxo_3Ppr8Y (Accessed 12 May 2020).

vate and public spaces, and to the implicit and explicit rules that women must abide in order to succeed in such spaces. The images of kitchens from the Epic Kitchens dataset are private spaces. For us, the power in this work is in the juxtaposition of texts that bring those images of the private realm into the public domain as conversations about women's domestic and commercial kitchen experiences.

Woolf's extended essay, 'A Room of One's Own', explores women's creative production, the need for equal access to education, and how having a room for oneself and their own money can allow women the time and autonomy to create. For many women across time, the kitchen has been her space, and while it may have been a shared space, it was the place for her to express her creativity, albeit often coinciding with the unpaid labor of caring for herself and her family. In recent decades women have also had more access to culinary training and work in professional kitchens, but for many this has come with the steep cost of feeling pressured to conform to the culture of the old boys' club mentality, or being subjected to terrible acts of sexual harassment or assault. We chose to honor Woolf's feminist canonical text with our project, and in doing so, we also took on the laboursome task of "prepping" the videos; a work that seems invisible in the final result yet akin to preparing food in domestic spaces.

A Kitchen of One's Own, like its spin-off *Epic Hand Washing in a Time of Lost Narratives*, is a remix of two sets of data, however the scope of the original project is much larger.

After burrough, a professor of emerging media art, gathered 268 videos from the Epic Kitchens dataset – a

task that took three weeks of continuous download-
ing – she created a prototype of how she imagined the
final project to appear on the Media Wall. With a set
of videos edited to 30 second clips, she brought a series
of grid designs to technical director Dale MacDonald,
Associate Dean of Creative Technologies in the University of Texas at Dallas, in search of an easier way
to generate the videos in the square format and thirty
second duration she would need for display. MacDonald wrote a script in Python to extract keyframe data7
from the original videos. By plotting timecodes in each
video where nouns and verbs had been tagged, he then
exported thirty-second video clips using an applica-
tion called FFMpeg.

Collectively, we spent more time processing video
for this project than any other task, as some of the
original videos in the Epic Kitchens dataset were up
to 1 hour in length. *In A Kitchen of One's Own* the
55 hours of footage from the 'Epic' dataset resulted
in a transformation of those original 268 videos
into 6,560 unique thirty-second clips, where the
keyframe that holds the verb/noun tag data appears
at the end of the video file. MacDonald created
the javascript code that randomly arranges videos
into one of burrough's grid formations and sets the

---

7   A keyframe is a single frame associated with a specific timecode during
time-based media, such as animation or video, where an action takes
place. In simplest form, one might assign three keyframes to the movement "jump" – the first keyframe when the jumper is on the ground,
the second at the top of the jump (midair), and the last on the ground
again. In the Epic Kitchens dataset, the keyframe data is a specific timecode that has been used to tag the video with language. Over time, the
tagged verbs or nouns repeat on certain types of images. This human
labour aids the programming of machine learning.

quote across the whole of the media wall. As seen in
IMG 8 and IMG 9, the typography is set in selected
typefaces for literature, journalism, and social media.
The verbs originally assigned by the Epic Kitchens
researchers and the selected literary quotes we present
in this project create an invitation for the viewer to
reimagine the kitchen performances as narratives
written by or about women across time and culture.
A final text box appears at the top of the wall to
display the verb that was assigned to the videos on
the monitors, and that the collaborators also applied
to quotes in the textual dataset.

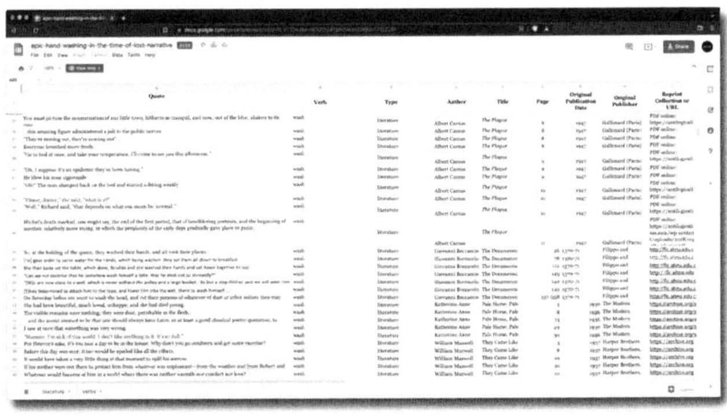

A Kitchen of One's Own, textual dataset, burrough and Starnaman,
screenshot, March 2020. The same set of verbs used by Epic Kitchens
researchers are assigned to each quote in the database. <⌀5>

The textual dataset of *A Kitchen of One's Own* includes more than 140 quotes from three categories:
literature, social media, and journalism. Starnaman, a
literature professor, with Alyssa Yates, a research assistant, sourced these quotes working together, using their
human (not machine) vision to identify selections that
captured women's experience in a concise way. This

was a job that required poetic discernment and semantic insight to identify textual selections that would resonate with human experience and offer creative spaces for viewers to create imaginative links. Starnaman and Yates also searched Twitter, and British and American news sources for articles about sexual assault and harrassment in all manner of professional kitchens. Many of these texts were written from first person points of view or featured extensive interviews with survivors of assault. Not surprisingly, reading about #MeToo in professional kitchens often left them feeling, more than ever, the need for a kitchen of one's own.

Quarantined In Our Kitchens

At this moment of writing in May 2020, we are still quarantined in our homes. Our Governor has declared that Dallas is in "Phase 1" of re-opening, but neither of us believe it is safe to live like we did before the pandemic began. So we continue to stay at home, and move primarily between the bedroom, living room, outside space, and kitchen – with the greatest day time spent in the kitchen preparing meals, cleaning, and working at the kitchen table. Our excitement about completing *A Kitchen of One's Own* was tempered by our sustained foray into the readings of women's experiences in commercial kitchens. However, developing *Epic Hand Washing in a Time of Lost Narratives* has given us a way to imagine this as a time that is not lost, but full of narrative possibility. Moreover, with this project we enter into the larger global conversation emerging around how to make sense of this generation-defining time; a conversation that will continue for a long time.

Hyperlinks

<&1>   https://unthinking.photography/
        projects/epichandwashing/
<&2>   https://epic-kitchens.github.io/2019
<&3>   https://en.wikipedia.org/
        wiki/On_Being_Ill
<&4>   https://drive.google.com/
        file/d/1hSV-91_ETTOruBpI-
        NCOChjuPtprlZue/view?usp=sharing
<&5>   https://forms.gle/Z8deJkyM28wCa3ADA

On Lacework: watching an entire machine-learning dataset

Everest Pipkin

This text, originally commissioned for Unthinking Photography, accompanied the work *Lacework* by Everest Pipkin as part of the Data/Set/Match programme at The Photographers' Gallery in 2020. Lacework was a new work by Pipkin that used artificial neural networks to reinscribe the videos of MIT's *Moments in Time Dataset*. Due to Covid-19 measures, the work was presented online from the 30th of June, and then, when the conditions allowed, it was shown on The Photographers' Gallery Media Wall from the 1st until the 31st of October 2020.

I proposed what would become *Lacework* in the summer of 2019. In my proposal, I describe a cycle of videos curated from MIT's *Moments in Time* dataset, each then slowed down, interpolated, and upscaled immensely into imagined detail, one flowing into another like a river.

In many ways, *Moments in Time* is unremarkable. Like so many datasets with similar goals, *Moments in Time* is intended to train AI systems to recognise actions. It contains one million 3-second videos scraped from websites like YouTube and Flickr, each tagged with a single verb like "asking", "resting", "snowing" or "praying".

There are a few things that are particular about *Moments in Time*. It tries to break down *most possi-*

ble actions into just 339 "doing" verbs. It also doesn't clarify the subjects of its videos – for instance, it is more interested in that something is flying than if that thing is a bee, a flower, a person, a plane, a satellite, or a bird. *Moments in Time* decentres human actions in favour of how words might apply to broader swaths of "doing".

Because these decisions require a particular type of logic, the language of this research is oddly poetic. The associated whitepaper reads:[1] "three seconds is a temporal envelope which holds meaningful actions between people, objects and phenomena"; and "visual and auditory events can be symmetrical in time ('opening' is 'closing' in reverse), and either transient or sustained."

One million videos is not a particularly large archive in the world of big data, but it is still a number meant for machine comprehension, not human. The first time I opened the dataset I got dizzy. One million moments, placed in folders named simply: sleeping, slicing, sliding, smelling, smiling. I felt like I'd been placed down somewhere on the surface of the earth, and told to walk home.

Without a methodology, I began haphazardly moving through the folders, dipping into specific verbs, pulling up a few dozen random videos until I found one that I liked. This was enough to test the aesthetic process through which I would approach the work, but did lit-

---

1   Monfort, M., Zhou, B., Bargal, S.A., Andonian, A., Yan, T., Ramakrishnan, K., Brown, L., Fan, Q., Gutfreund, D., Vondrick, C., & Oliva, A. (2020) 'Moments in Time Dataset: One Million Videos for Event Understanding'. *IEEE Transactions on Pattern Analysis and Machine Intelligence*, 42, pp. 502-508. Available at: https://arxiv.org/pdf/1801.03150.pdf (Accessed 20 July 2020).

tle to teach me about the structure of the dataset itself. It was not until I entered quarantine in March 2020, months after I'd begun, that this process moved from a random selection to a deliberate and focused one.

When the pandemic moved the project online, I considered focusing on videos about touch, that subject that had been transmuted from a casual action to a precious and dangerous one. I pulled roughly 20 folders from the archive by verb: cuddling, hugging, punching, and reaching. These folders still contained 60,000 videos between them, but this was a scale that I felt was possible to approach, as one person stuck in a room.

As the world entombed, I spent my time watching these short, tiny moments of intimacy – two lovebirds beak to beak, a tiger putting paws around a keeper, the contact of a fist to a face, a kiss, a crowd, a touch.

I was looking for videos with a lot of texture to them, with subjects at a distance, in shapes or colours that were already confusing. I wanted compositions that the AI upscaling could catch onto and drag against, pulling a cloud into a mountain or a face into a coastline.

Somehow, I had expected the act of watching *Moments in Time* to be calming or exploratory, like seeing the world out of a window. But the archive is not entertaining, poetic, beautiful, or joyful, even though many videos that evoke those feelings are contained within it. It is an archive with purpose, an archive of actions for an inhuman eye. Here is the world, here are things that are done there. It feels raw.

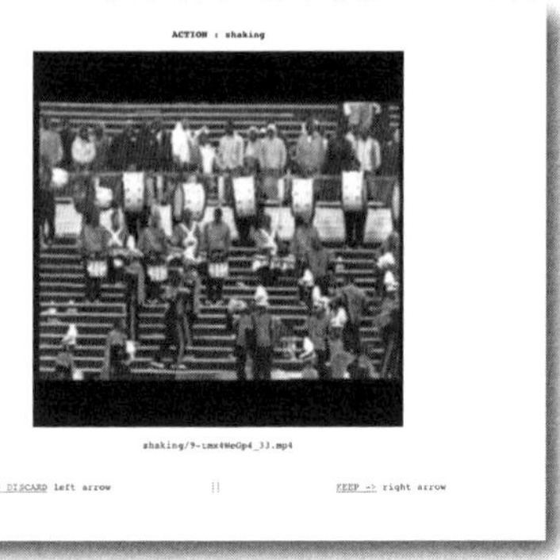

My own, handmade selection interface

Eventually, I built myself a Tinder-like interface for screening the videos. Each video would pop up and I would then tap the left or right arrow key to sort it into place: *Yes* or *No*, keep or throw away.

Out of these 60,000 videos I selected roughly 400. I slowed each one down dramatically, drawing the video out to 15 seconds from its original three-seconds duration. I interpolated the frames, attempting to make a new flowing motion to replace the smoothness lost in the time conversion. I wanted to be able to study these moments intended to teach machines what it is to touch. I wanted to see each small choice in each body taking action, removed from human time.

It was now early April 2020. I had watched 6% of the dataset, about 50 hours of videos, and from them had made a little over an hour of material.

I could have stopped there. But I kept thinking about the rest of the archive – all those other verbs, all this other life. I felt that the videos around touch were not enough of the story. They didn't say enough about what the dataset was trying to do, what it contained.

I decided I needed to watch the rest of the dataset. This time I started at the top, alphabetically.

Aiming, applauding, arresting, ascending, asking.

Last fall, when we could still gather in rooms together, I taught a class called 'Data Gardens'. One of the units was around performance as AI. We talked about "Wizard of Oz prototyping" <🔗1> and human labour in machine-learning systems. We watched movies of actors pretending to be androids, replicants, and machines. We looked at histories of automata, including the miraculous 18th-century chess-playing Mechanical Turk, which in reality hid a petite human chess master among its clockwork.

When I first started watching the dataset I assumed that the team of researchers who had put it together at MIT had seen the bulk of it, but I'm now convinced that assumption was wrong. This is because so much of the archive is so, so hard to watch.

This is partly to do with time. The videos in *Moments in Time* have a severe, automated cut (3 seconds, sharp) that severs these moments, sometimes chopping them in the middle of the action that they are meant to describe. I eventually found that I had to mute the videos in order to keep watching at all. The images could dissolve into colours and shapes but the jarring severance of the sound remained distinct and pointed no matter how much I watched.

The difficulty of watching is also partly to do with consent. *Moments in Time* severs the relationship between recorded action and original maker. The researchers did not ask for permission to use these videos, and all ownership of – and control over – the image is pulled away from the person who held the camera, and from what that camera depicts.

In the archive, there are moments of extreme emotion and personal vulnerability – tears, screaming, and pain. Moments of questionable consent, including pornography. Racist and fascist imagery. Animal cruelty and torture. And worse; I saw horrible images. I saw dead bodies. I saw human lives end.

Even though I'm probably the first person to watch *all* of *Moments in Time*, every part of the dataset has had human eyes on it before. This is because after being gathered and cut, the videos of *Moments in Time* were automatically uploaded to Amazon Mechanical Turk for annotation. Amazon Mechanical Turk is a crowdsourcing service that connects "requesters" to "workers" who generally perform small, computer-like tasks for pennies. It is owned by Amazon and takes its name from the fake chess-playing machine.

The *Moments in Time* whitepaper describes the process of annotating the videos:

"Each AMT worker is presented with a video-verb pair and asked to press a Yes or No key signifying if the action is happening in the scene. Positive responses from the first round are sent to subsequent rounds of annotation. Each HIT (a single worker assignment) contains 64 different 3-second videos that are related to a single verb."

I'm reminded of my own years spent as an AMT worker, which kept me employed at well under minimum wage during, and after, my undergraduate education. I think about all those thousands of tasks, which involved the repetition of my labour. Hitting buttons with my hands, matching emotions with my face, recording words with my voice. How many datasets my body must be contained in. What those datasets are used for. How much violence my body does to others, through them.

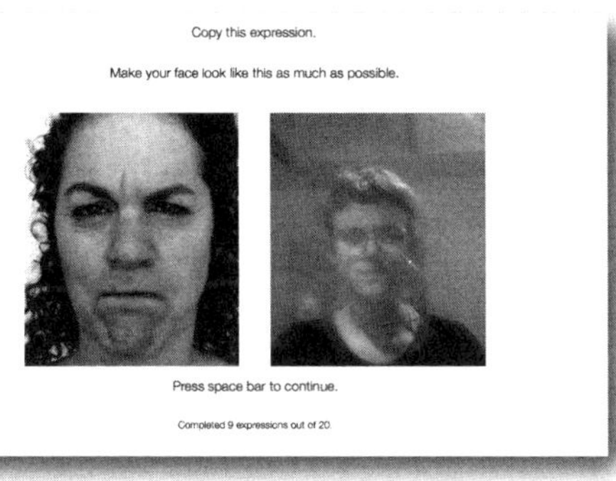

Me (right), in 2013, training a facial recognition database on Amazon Mechanical Turk for roughly $4 an hour.

The example interface described by the *Moments in Time* whitepaper has an unsettling resemblance to my own handmade video-screening method, with the right and left arrow keys standing in for Yes and No. Both contain only two options: include, discard. No ability to report a video, reclassify it or clarify its inclusion, no middle ground.

It comes to explain the brutality within.

When you ask:

Does a dog fight match "barking"?

Does a sexual assault match "kissing"?

Does a police murder match "arresting"?

Sometimes the answer is Yes.

Around hour 250 of the dataset, sometime in late

April, I started having The Dream. In The Dream I am living on – or perhaps *am* – a research satellite, orbiting a planet and monitoring planetary broadcasts. For each brief moment I am floating over a place, I can see just a flash of what is happening under me. Just a fleeting, tiny vision of *something happening* then *something happening* then *something happening*. The dream goes on this way for years.

Even awake, I've come to see patterns in camera quality, in shadows, in the colour of paint and the types of trees, in movement, in texture that could unfold into ever more detail. I see patterns in everything, patterns that unify all of the videos which have nothing to do with their subjects and everything to do with the way the lens sweeps up to capture a running dog, or pivots to see the sunset or the way the light flares and the compression pushes against the edges of the frame.

I wonder if this is how a sorting algorithm feels.

By now, I am running the upscaling algorithm parallel to my own curatorial work. My computer hums and struggles as it processes and reprocesses images, imagining detail where there is none – from 80 pixels to 160, from 160 to 320, 320 to 640, and finally to 1280, all full of imagined detail.

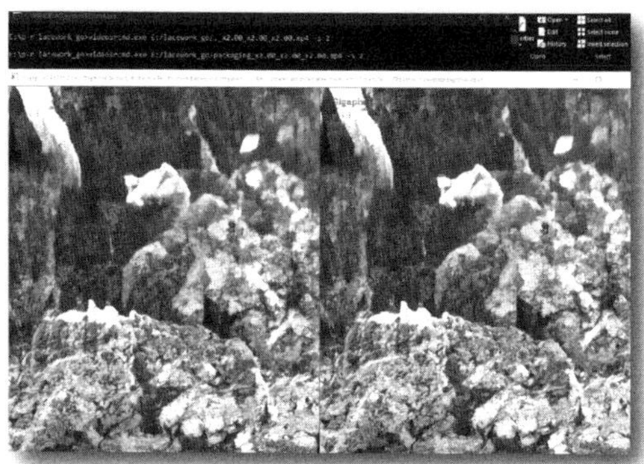

The Topaz Lab upscaling software running
as a batch process.

I'm using Topaz Lab's proprietary software *AI Gigapixel* to do the bulk of the upscaling, which is wrapped in an easy to use command-line interface. It was trained on yet another dataset of pictures at various resolutions. It sees patterns too. This process has been described as hallucinatory, which is an accurate marker — it is a recurrent looking, a push in and in, for ever more detail, which then spirals into something else entirely.

Like looking at images of the earth via satellite.

See IMG 11 on page 186
See IMG 12 on page 187

By the point that I am halfway through the dataset in early May 2020, I am running out of time. I start spending whole days in the archive, watching from the moment I wake up to when I go to sleep. I'm this far, and I want to do it right. The act of watching itself has become important to me.

In this archive of actions, I want to perform action. I become grateful to wake up every day knowing how I will spend it. I'm not building a cathedral, but I think about what building a cathedral would let me do, how it would allow me to move my hands in a task and see something monumental grow very slowly, with immense care. A bricklayer understands brick in a way that is devotional.

Repetition is devotional.

Very slowly, over and over, my body learns the rules and edges of the dataset. I come to understand so much about it; how each source is structured, how the videos are found, the words that are caught in the algorithmic gathering.

I see the subjects of the videos, the people living their lives. I meet their dogs, I see their homes. I see wild animals, strange weather, places I'll never get to visit, video games I haven't played. I see so much life.

I can also see the hands of the person who held the camera, and the hands of the workers who first sorted the videos. These others who have also watched this exact moment, who had to decide before I did: Yes, or No.

I memorise qualities of the pattern; light, colour, noise, compression, blur, frame-rate. I know how these aspects will interact with the interpolation and the up-scaling. I don't have to think about it anymore – it is all automatic.

I learn the exact length of 3 seconds.

Every once in a while, in the satellite dream, there will be no broadcasts. I can't pick up anything – I just see the landscape that is underneath me, the mountains, the coastline. I can zoom the picture in, I can get closer, but all I see is world, not actions.

Sometimes I zoom in so far that I can see the lines in the dirt left by a tractor, by thousands of tractors, the ways in which they are interrupted by the boundaries of jagged creeks. I see the wind, the wind-formed dunes, the oil wells and the patterns they scar on the desert, the ocean, the wakes of boats, the wakes of islands. From above, the intertwined complexity of it all is so clear.

I see all these millions of lives, all of this infinite detail, this lacy intricacy that grows ever more granular the closer I get, then grows again, and again.

Hyperlinks

<&1>   https://en.wikipedia.org/wiki/
        Wizard_of_Oz_experiment

The Age of ImageNet's Discovery
Alan F. Blackwell

On the 10th anniversary of ImageNet, its creator Fei-Fei Li gave a talk at The Photographers' Gallery where she introduced the key people and events that led to the dataset's creation. Alan Blackwell chaired the talk. We asked him to reflect on Li's presentation as well as ImageNet and the current state of artificial intelligence (AI) more generally. As a response to our invitation, Blackwell proposed an essay drawing an analogy between the scientific discoveries being made in AI through the exploration of images retrieved from the Internet, and the early-modern "Age of Discovery". It considers the relations between the universalist epistemologies of cognitive science and the extractivist practices of artificial intelligence research.

Fei-Fei Li's engaging description of the development of ImageNet is a generous account of the contributions made by her many colleagues, telling a human story in which, as she says, "there is nothing artificial about artificial intelligence." As so often in scientific research, the human stories of discovery and exploration offer a fascinating insight into the paths that were followed to bring us to the knowledge we have today. The pace of change in digital technologies – subject to Moore's Law on the increase in computational power alongside the network effects driving the search engines and data repositories of the Internet – make the stories of AI discoveries especially exciting. When a project like ImageNet changes the way we see the world within a decade, the young researchers involved, like explorers 500 years ago during the early-modern "Age of Discovery", become celebrities early in their scientific careers. Fei-Fei Li uses that status with care, not only ensuring due credit to the collaborators and students who played important roles in the development of ImageNet, but in her more recent work as director of a centre dedicated to human-centred AI.

The story that Fei-Fei Li told in celebrating the 10th birthday of ImageNet also suggested other respects in which this work of discovery and exploration offers analogies to the Age of Discovery. This too is a human story. As in that earlier age, explorers bring with them scientific questions that reflect the concerns of the societies they come from. Those questions often appear different when seen from the perspective of earlier inhabitants, when explorers arrive in lands 'unknown to science', where their own maps might still be blank or sketchy. This essay discusses the differences in perspective between the human story of Fei-Fei Li and her colleagues, and other human stories in the "land" (the new territories and spaces of the Internet) that are being explored.

At the time of its 10th birthday party at The Photographers' Gallery, a degree of controversy had emerged around ImageNet, specifically in relation to the people who "lived there" – people whose photographs had become included in the ImageNet database. As with other voyages of discovery, this controversy arose in part from different ways of seeing this new territory: the scientific questions that motivated the expedition, in contrast to the perspectives and priorities of the "natives".

In the week immediately before Li's talk at the birthday celebration, press attention had been drawn to a project by Kate Crawford and Trevor Paglen. This involved their *Training Humans* exhibition in Milan, a critical essay on training sets for machine learning,[1] and the deployment of a demonstration app called *ImageNet Roulette.* Crawford and Paglen's key concerns relate to any system of classifying people, as explored for example in the classic text *Sorting Things Out* by science and technology scholars Geoff Bowker and Susan Leigh Star (2000).[2] As summarised by Crawford and Paglen, "much of the discussion around 'bias' in AI systems misses the mark: there is no 'neutral', 'natural', or 'apolitical' vantage point that training data can be built upon." However the *ImageNet Roulette* demonstration drew wider attention in particular because of the offensive terminology that had been encoded in the *WordNet* project – the project at Princeton that Li told us was the point of inspiration for ImageNet, providing its conceptual structure.[3]

WordNet, that port of departure for the ImageNet voyage of discovery, is certainly problematic, if not quixotic in its ambitions. George Miller, the initiator of WordNet, is famous as one of the founding figures of cognitive science, with contributions ranging from his

1   Crawford, K. and Paglen, T. (2019) *Excavating AI: The Politics of Training Sets for Machine Learning* [Online] Available at: https://www. excavating.ai (Accessed 26 March 2021).

2   Bowker, G. C., & Star, S. L. (2000) *Sorting things out: Classification and its consequences*, Cambridge, MA: MIT press.

3   Wong, J. C. (2019, September 18) 'The viral selfie app ImageNet Roulette seemed fun – until it called me a racist slur.' *The Guardian.* Available at: https://www.theguardian.com/technology/2019/sep/17/ imagenet-roulette-asian-racist-slur-selfie (Accessed 26 March 2021).

now-proverbial formulation of "the magic number seven, plus or minus two" in human perception and short-term memory,[4] to the field that he called *psycholexicology*, at the boundary of linguistics and psychology.[5] The ambition of WordNet, as with much cognitive science research, is to create models of meaning that are both universal (free of cultural elements) and compatible with computational representations. However, for most of the field's history, this 'universal' basis of mind and meaning has been taken to mean the educated understanding of the researchers themselves,[6] and of their WEIRD (Western, Educated, Industrialised, Rich and Democratic) experimental subjects.[7] Miller intended WordNet to be more than a thesaurus – indeed, a new kind of dictionary, indexed by meaning itself. The fact that this index of meaning includes demeaning gender assumptions, racially offensive terms, and many other unacceptable categories, makes it only too clear how problematic the apparently straightforward goals of WordNet became.

The ImageNet team have now responded to some of these more problematic aspects of the original Word-Net project by removing parts of the semantic index relating to people. The remaining sections of the dataset,

4   Miller, G. A. (1956) 'The magic number seven plus or minus two: Some limits on our capacity for processing information', *Psychological Review*, 63, pp. 91-97.

5   Miller, G. A., Beckwith, R., Fellbaum, C., Gross, D., & Miller, K. J. (1990) 'Introduction to WordNet: An on-line lexical database', *International Journal of Lexicography*, 3(4), pp. 235-244.

6   Forsythe, D. (2001) *Studying those who study us: An anthropologist in the world of artificial intelligence*. Stanford: Stanford University Press.

7   Henrich, J., Heine, S., & Norenzayan, A. (2010) 'The weirdest people in the world?', *Behavioral and Brain Sciences*, 33(2-3), pp. 61-83.

including non-human animals, objects and plants, are still a valuable resource for the engineering of computer vision systems, and it appears that decoupling the work from the epistemological foundations of cognitive science has done little harm to the prospects of deep neural networks for practical applications. Of course, the rhetoric of AI does continue to rely on presumed analogies between the structure of these systems and the human mind (the term "neural network" being only one among many that allows misleading equivalences to be drawn)[8]. Fei-Fei Li, as with many researchers in this field, began her career as a cognitive scientist before becoming an engineer. However, her talk made clear how much of the actual work in constructing ImageNet did not involve experimental studies of the human mind, but rather the managerial processes of commissioning labelling work via Amazon Mechanical Turk (coordinated by her student Jia Deng),[9] and coordinating competition entries in the *ImageNet Large Scale Visual Recognition Challenge* (the work of her student Olga Russakovsky).[10]

Many fields of computer science engineering research are driven forward by benchmarking challenges, in which a standardised set of tests is defined, including quantitative measures of performance in completing them. Bench-

8   Agre, P. E. (1997) 'Towards a Critical Technical Practice: Lessons Learned in Trying to Reform AI'. in: Bowker, G. Star, S. L & Turner, W. (Eds) *Social Science, Technical Systems and Cooperative Work*, Lawrence Erlbaum, Mahwah, NJ, pp. 131-157.

9   Deng, J., Dong, W., Socher, R., Li, L. J., Li, K., & Fei-Fei, L. (2009) 'Imagenet: A large-scale hierarchical image database', Proc. IEEE conference on computer vision and pattern recognition (CVPR), pp. 248-255.

10   Russakovsky, O., Deng, J., Su, H. et al. (2015) 'ImageNet Large Scale Visual Recognition Challenge', *International Journal of Computer Vision 115*, pp.211-252. Available at: https://doi.org/10.1007/s11263-015-0816-y (Accessed 10 May 2023).

mark challenges provide a common metric by which alternative algorithms (or hardware implementations) can be objectively compared. Technical conferences in many subfields of computer science include benchmark competitions that can be used to assess which approaches are most successful and which research teams are the most skilled. The most influential benchmarks (such as the Text REtrieval Conference TREC) implicitly define the central concerns of a whole academic field, while manufacturers, research consortia and large laboratories are keen to ensure that new benchmarks favour their own products or research agendas.

The successful launch of the ImageNet Challenge was thus a pivotal moment in the ImageNet story. Benchmark challenges have a particularly interesting status in the case of machine learning research: the challenge definition includes not only a set of performance tests (as with any benchmark) but also a standardised set of training data, in order to ensure an even playing field for all the learning algorithms that are entered. However, commercial advances in machine learning have become more reliant on the quality of the training data than on variations in the algorithm – the convolutional neural network approach was already well-known, and even considered old-fashioned, before the dramatic success achieved after it had been trained with the ImageNet data. The large investment in constructing the ImageNet *dataset* was thus an essential prerequisite for adoption of the ImageNet *challenge*, but resulted in a game where the leaders of the ImageNet project effectively played the roles of both coach and umpire.

Other groups had previously constructed training and benchmark datasets for image classification, including the *PASCAL Visual Object Classes* (VOC) challenges, and the *CIFAR-10* and *CIFAR-100* subsets of the *tiny image* dataset originally collected by researchers at MIT and NYU. This is a small and tight-knit research community. As mentioned in her talk, Li's first good quality scientific publication came from her visit to the Oxford group that managed the VOC challenge, while the *tiny image* team included Rob Fergus, who had shared his Master's degree group with Fei-Fei Li at CalTech, before moving to that same Oxford group for his PhD. As with any other community of explorers, groups such as these acquire and define shared understanding of their goals; a common theme across all of these groups was the need for some kind of systematics in the labelling of objects. In the case of VOC, "The classes can be considered in a notional taxonomy" (divided into vehicles, household items, animals, and "other" – a superclass that revealingly contains only one entry: "person"). ImageNet and *tiny images* have even more in common, in that both are based on the semantic hierarchy of WordNet. Indeed, following the critique of these categories by Paglen and Crawford,[11] and then by Prabhu and Birhane,[12] the tiny images dataset has been withdrawn from public view or usage as of June 2020 (see Torralba et al).[13]

11   Crawford, K. and Paglen, T. (2019) *Excavating AI: The Politics of Training Sets for Machine Learning* [Online] Available at: https://www. excavating.ai (Accessed 26 March 2021).

12   Prabhu, V. U. and Birhane, A. (2020) 'Large image datasets: A pyrrhic win for computer vision?' [Online] Available at: https://arxiv.org/ abs/2006.16923 (Accessed 26 March 2021).

13   Torralba, A., Fergus, R., & Freeman, W. T. (2020) Untitled notice dated June 29th, 2020: "It has been brought to our attention…" http:// groups.csail.mit.edu/vision/TinyImages/ (Accessed 26 March 2021).

In addition to sharing the same kind of taxonomic navigation aids, this tight-knit band of explorers were also constructing their conceptual maps to describe the same territory – the set of all images that could be obtained (for free) from the Internet. Yet it is interesting to ask what other human stories are involved, beyond those of the scientific teams, when exploring this territory. Who are the metaphorical porters, bearers or guides for the expeditions in this modern Age of Discovery? Internet users might be considered to be the people recruited to label the images, providing the categorising "intelligence" that can later be mined, extracted and processed in order for an AI to replicate their judgments. In publications describing the datasets, as in Li's talk, researchers describe the challenges of working with such users. The people creating the labels were not so much the focus of the human story told by Fei-Fei Li (none of these characters have names), although they do often seem to appear at the centre of the action. Rob Fergus' team, like Li's, complain that undergraduates are too slow and costly,[14] while the Oxford group finds that workers on Amazon Mechanical Turk are too unreliable.[15]

Fortunately, another source of intelligence was available for free, just as with the minerals, animal life or veg-

14   Torralba, A., Fergus, R., & Freeman, W. T. (2008) '80 million tiny images: A large data set for nonparametric object and scene recognition,' IEEE Transactions on Pattern Analysis and Machine Intelligence (PAMI), 30(11), pp. 1958-1970.

15   Everingham, M., Eslami, S.M.A., Van Gool, L., Williams, C.K.I., Winn, J. and Zisserman, A. (2015) 'The PASCAL Visual Object Classes Challenge: A Retrospective', *International Journal of Computer Vision*, 111(1), pp. 98-136. Available at: http://host.robots.ox.ac.uk/pascal/VOC/pubs/everingham15.pdf (Accessed 26 March 2021).

etation that might be found lying around by colonisers of an unknown territory (setting aside the question of whether indigenous people might have views about the ownership of these things). This additional source of intelligence is behind the hand that aims the camera, and the eye that composes the image – in short, the intelligence of the photographer. As Fei-Fei Li spoke at The Photographers' Gallery in London, many in the audience would be alert to the work that must be invested in these apparently "natural" images, in order for them to become a coherent and readable representation of "dog", "airplane" or any other semantic category in one of the training datasets. Since the photographer's own intelligence has been embedded in each image through their labour, it is worth attending to the ways that "artificial intelligence" is created by mining the supposedly raw materials of intelligence found for free on the Internet. As Li says in her introduction, "there is nothing artificial in artificial intelligence", because all of this intelligence can be traced to human people, whether or not their names were recorded.

How did this metaphorical "land" of the whole Internet – the greatest repository of human intelligence ever created – become available for mining as if it were unknown territory being explored for the first time? The images of real people, which were so obviously problematic when categorised as "sluts" or "alcoholics" by WordNet, were not a simple consequence of surveillance capitalism, the accidental data exhaust created as a contractual by-product of people's online shopping or music playlists.[16] It is quite clear that the people being

16   Zuboff, S. (2019) *The Age of Surveillance Capitalism: The fight for a human future at the new frontier of power*, London: Profile Books.

photographed had not consented to participate in scientific research (or, indeed, to be featured in a gallery exhibition).[17] Those failures of governance must surely be attributed to the way that principles of consent have been eroded by the fatuous end-user licence agreements of online platforms, through which there is now little expectation of natural justice, leading to apathy and resignation on the part of Internet users who click "Accept" without even reading the terms.[18]

This essay has drawn several parallels between scientific exploitation of the cultural commons of the Internet, and the historical agenda of science in relation to indigenous people and their land during the so-called "Age of Discovery". Most readers will have been uncomfortably aware of the aftermath of that supposedly heroic age, in which arguments from science were developed and deployed to construct theories of race in an attempt to justify slavery and settler colonialism.[19] When we look back at those origins, the actions and attitudes of the explorers can already be recognised as the seeds of subsequent atrocities. Importantly, I do not suggest that there is an equivalence between the acts of a few, even if foolish or despicable from today's perspective, and the industrial scales of slaughter and exploitation that followed.

17   Lyons, M. (2020, December 24) 'Excavating "Excavating AI": The Elephant in the Gallery.' [Online] Available at: https://arxiv.org/pdf/2009.01215.pdf (Accessed 26 March 2021).

18   Luger, E., Moran, S., & Rodden, T. (2013) 'Consent for all: revealing the hidden complexity of terms and conditions'. In *Proceedings of the SIGCHI conference on human factors in computing systems*, pp. 2687-2696.

19   Saini, A. (2019) *Superior: the return of race science*, Boston, MA: Beacon Press.

Nevertheless, from this perspective, the parallels drawn in relation to the conduct of science in different eras should stir disturbing resonances, in considering what might come next. The seeds of future industries must surely be significant, even if history is determined on longer timescales. I have not, in this essay, investigated the ways in which AI research itself is a product of earlier waves of racist science and the legacies of slavery and settler colonialism. Those questions are a serious concern for AI research, although others are writing on this topic with far more insight and rigour than I do myself. I strongly hope that the more speculative analogy that I have investigated here does not detract from those more urgent and important problems. New work in this field is rapidly being amassed, but I particularly draw attention to recent publications by Shakir Mohamed et al.,[20] by Abeba Birhane,[21] by Rachel Adams,[22] by Stephen Cave[23] and by Ruha Benjamin,[24] for those who wish to understand further how AI is fundamentally racist, and to see the potential consequences – for centuries to come – of scientific enquiries that fail to engage with their ethical suppositions and shortcomings.

20   Mohamed, S., Png, M. T., & Isaac, W. (2020) 'Decolonial AI: Decolonial theory as sociotechnical foresight in artificial intelligence', *Philosophy & Technology*, 33(4), pp. 659-684.

21   Birhane, A. (2020) 'Algorithmic colonization of Africa', *SCRIPTed*, 17, p.389.

22   Adams, R. (2021) 'Can artificial intelligence be decolonised?', *Interdisciplinary Science Reviews*, 46, 1-2: Artificial Intelligence & its discontents, https://doi.org/10.1080/03080188.2020.1840225.

23   Cave, S. (2020) 'The problem with intelligence: its value-laden history and the future of AI'. In *Proceedings of the AAAI/ACM Conference on AI, Ethics, and Society*, pp. 29-35.

24   Benjamin, R. (2019) *Race after technology: abolitionist tools for the new Jim code*, Medford, MA: Polity.

The economic inequalities of the gig economy, of "crowd sourcing" micro-labour, "ReCAPTCHA" labelling tasks as the price of entry to public spaces, and other sources of ghost labour, have not yet recapitulated the crimes and gross inequalities of slavery and settler colonialism that resulted from the voyages of exploration during the Age of Discovery. But we should certainly be concerned that the "raw material" of artificial intelligence – the whole content of the Internet – is actually creative human work, alienated from its creators through intellectual property law that has not only failed to realise the public benefits of the Creative Commons as originally envisioned by Lawrence Lessig,[25] but appears to have legitimised monopolistic exploitation by the mass media rentiers of our shared cultural heritage.[26]

The land being explored in artificial intelligence research is, in one important way, not like those geographies where new knowledge and technology were used to extract resources. In this metaphorical land of scientific discovery, the natural resources being extracted from the Internet are not animal, vegetable or mineral, but the material of people's own intelligence. Is the mining of the Internet to turn natural into "artificial" intelligence a ruse to bypass Article 27 of the Universal Declaration of Human Rights, evading that legal commitment to recognition and protection of au-

25 Lessig, L. (2008) *Remix: Making art and commerce thrive in the hybrid economy*, London: Penguin.

26 Schwartz, J. (2004) 'Will Mickey be property of Disney forever? Divergent attitudes toward patent and copyright extensions in light of Eldred v. Ashcroft', *University of Illinois Journal of Law, Technology and Policy*, 1, pp. 105-128.

thorship in images and other creative works? If the un-explored territories of the Internet were ever a Creative Commons, it would appear that the construction of AI datasets, and the systems built from them, may represent yet another Enclosure of the Commons.

From Spectacle to Extraction.
And All Over Again

Gaia Tedone

This text was originally commissioned as a video interview between Gaia Tedone and Kate Crawford and Trevor Paglen on the occasion of their exhibition *Training Humans* at Osservatorio Prada in Milan. It was published on Unthinking Photography in November 2019 as part of the Data/Set/Match programme at The Photographer's Gallery. This essay is a rework of the text specifically for the purpose of this publication.

I met with Kate Crawford and Trevor Paglen at the press preview of their exhibition *Training Humans* in Milan at Osservatorio Prada. It was the morning of September 11th – not a neutral day to unthink photography and the power operations of vast populations of images. On the contrary, it was the most apt day to seriously consider Crawford and Paglen's proposition that "images are no longer spectacle but they are in fact looking back at us, being actors in a process of massive value extraction."

The show was a highly anticipated one, being the result of a two-year collaborative project which saw Kate Crawford (NYU research professor and co-founder of the AI Now Institute in New York) and Trevor Paglen (internationally renowned artist, researcher and recipient of multiple prizes) engaged in opening the so-called black box of AI. Their different disciplinary orientations converged around questions of what an image is in AI systems, who gets to decide its meaning and for what purposes. These issues echo old questions that photography criticism has dealt with for decades, which today need urgent revising – both in terms of their formulations and answers. This is particularly in light of the epistemological challenges computer vision and artificial intelligence are bringing to the wider infrastructures of meaning. I got ready to train myself to see what was lying inside the black box of AI – inside the white cube of Osservatorio Prada.

At the beginning of the press conference, Crawford and Paglen kicked off with a joke about how any conversation about AI inevitably starts with the CIA and some cruel cat experiments. They were referring to the material on display on the first floor of the exhibition: leaked documents from the facial recognition project financed by the CIA and carried out by Woodrow Wilson Bledsoe in 1963, and some footage from Colin Blakemore's experiments on cats undertaken in the 1970s when studying the animals' visual cortex. This material served to bring a historical perspective to the main issue at stake: how both humans and non-humans see. AI is not a new business. Neither is vision. There is a history behind it and even a pre-history (or archaeology) to it, as Crawford and Paglen rightly point out, which involves centuries of experiments and trials at the crossover between science, technology, and creative practices.

Similarly, this project does not come out of the blue. It emerges out of a specific historical moment – one that we might refer to as "image capitalism"[1] or "platform capitalism"[2] or "computational capitalism"[3] – and in response to an emergent field of practice. This field is populated by a number of artists-researchers-practitioners who are preoccupied, much like Crawford and Paglen, with the social, ethical and political implications of AI and the materiality of its computer vision algorithms. This is a point that needs to be made, as Crawford and Paglen lament an insufficient presence of critical inquiry towards these issues, whilst gracefully taking up the role of "AI ambassadors" within the so-called institutional art establishment. However, a survey of current creative practices engaged with the algorithms of machine learning was never really on Crawford and Paglen's agenda, nor would it have made an interesting exhibition.

The show's archaeological approach had a greater urgency in order to situate an emerging set of image practices. Its ambition was to rethink the fraught relationship between an image and a label in training sets, as we move from a regime of spectacle to one of extraction, under a new political economy of meaning-making, whose lexicon and syntax is being built by the AI industry.

These were some of the issues we discussed on an improvised stage set on the second floor of the exhi-

1   Mbembe, A. (2011) *'The Dream of Safety'. Figures and Fictions Conference.* Victoria and Albert Museum Lecture. Available at: at:http://dreamofsafety.blogspot.co.uk/2011/07/achille-mbembes-lecture-at-victoria-and.html. (Accessed 10 February 2021).

2   Srnicek, N. (2017) *Platform Capitalism*, Cambridge: Polity Press.

3   Beller, J. (2016) 'The Programmable Image of Capital: M-I-C-I-M', *Postmodern Culture*, 26 (2). DOI:10.1353/PMC.2016.0005.

bition space at Osservatorio Prada. Crawford and Paglen sat on two poufs we borrowed from the nearby "instagrammable" installation *ImageNet Roulette*. There, all of us visiting the exhibition sat in front of two screens with cameras and put our faces and bodies up for scrutiny. In the presence of the algorithmic oracle, we waited, amused, for our ages, genders, and professions to be detected and labelled. The images from the installation were predictably posted back on social media, particularly on Instagram, where the hashtag #imagenetroutlette quickly gained traction, spreading the popularity of the show, of its two "celebrity creators" and of Fondazione Prada.

See IMG 13 on page 188

Was this a game or a serious game, to say it with Harun Farocki? Perhaps it was spectacle, desperately attempting to smuggle itself back in the vicious cycle of algorithmic extraction. After all, the two – spectacle and extraction – seem intimately related to me, as Art meets AI at the interface of the networked image. Unlike in any other show, here the networked image blatantly performed its dual role as a computational structure and as an interface for visual communication.

With the duo's back set against the backdrop of some flickering screens and a wallpaper of images drawn from one of the datasets on display – the *Selfie dataset* – we began our conversation.[4] I was interested in hear-

---

4   The video interviews undertaken by Gaia Tedone can be viewed on
     Unthinking Photography or watched as a playlist on YouTube: https://
     youtube.com/playlist?list=PLshWAoHIYAsnFbd6uKIZ14nG0NW
     3SOwGl.

ing the genealogy of their collaborative project and the research questions that animated this joint enterprise.

The conversation flowed as Crawford and Paglen unpacked the title of the show and the concept of "predator vision of AI" – one that is key to their proposition of AI as a value-extracting industry that is making fundamental interventions into the very fabric of contemporary visual culture.

They then moved on to explain what is really at stake when attempting to read and critically interpret datasets, underlining the racial and gender biases inscribed in the process of labelling and classifying images into discrete categories. They talked about the subtle gradient between description and judgement, and the power operations at play as meaning gets codified into images whilst images are, by all means, computational code.

I enquired about the importance of ImageNet within the historical trajectory of training datasets that the exhibition traces. Crawford and Paglen specifically touched upon the question of human labour and the use of Amazon Mechanical Turk workers: how this emerged as a defining trait of ImageNet's monumental effort at providing the most comprehensive and diverse coverage of the image world.

We then moved on to one of the most controversial aspects of the project: the ethical issues involved in putting this kind of material on display without people's previous awareness nor consent. In other words, Crawford and Paglen's choice, or "bet", as they describe it, to reproduce at the level of the exhibition the same intrusion into people's lives and privacy as AI performs when trained algorithms scrape images from social media accounts and online spaces. Their answer was well prepped – they explained that there is a structure in place by which visitors of the show can have their images removed, if they want to, and pondered why we, as humans, should see any differently than machines. With this provocation, they implied that privacy is breached in the first place by the very process of putting together these datasets in order to train machine learning algorithms.

What they failed to recognise though, as commentators and critics of the show have subsequently highlighted, is that this was not always the case.[5] There are key considerations of context to account for as the anatomy of these training sets is disclosed to a wider audience, including the role and consent of the participants, or whether a given dataset was scraped from the Internet or constructed. In other words, when attempting to frame datasets as 'cultural objects', one cannot separate them from the particular historical moment and conditions they emerged from, and the specific computational problem they were built to tackle.

More questions arose in my mind: as these images are put on display in an art gallery, don't they revert back to the status of spectacle? How can we think critically about circulation and its relation to the new political economy of meaning making? What networks of power are involved in this process of circulation, as images travel from computer labs to social media and art galleries, and back into tech labs? Isn't the ex-

<hr>

5   Lyons, M. (2020, December 24) Excavating "Excavating AI": The Elephant in the Gallery. [Online] Available at: https://arxiv.org/pdf/2009.01215.pdf (Accessed 10 February 2021).

hibition ultimately replicating the same mechanisms Crawford and Paglen are criticising?

These questions can be addressed to all art projects grappling with the politics of dataset representation, including the ones presented in 2019 on the Media Wall of The Photographers' Gallery as part of the programme Data/Set/Match. When it comes to having a 'real conversation' about the politics of dataset representation, one might wonder if the exhibition is actually the most apt format and the institutional art establishment the most eligible contender. The latter, in fact, comes with its own set of filters, biases and opaque dynamics as the imperative of audience metrics coalesce with that of institutional branding, and the packaging of exhibitions and theoretical ideas. However, this show crucially pointed out that tracing the networks of circulation of these images in and off the Web might reveal a great deal about the new political economy of meaning in the time of AI – one shaped by the operations of users, algorithms, platforms and complex computational systems.

My final question concerned the politics of archiving and the issue of training datasets vanishing from the Internet. This question was meant to provoke a reflection about the current state of affairs; one characterised by a race towards "cleaning up" the Internet from what has started to be seen as highly controversial material. Training sets are vanishing overnight, perhaps risking the erasure of an important piece of AI history that, in spite of its errors and mistakes, could produce a roadmap for future development in the field. Crawford and Paglen's view on the topic was thoughtful, as this is something the two have discussed at length while writing the article *Excavating AI. The*

Politics of Images in Machine Learning Training Sets,[6] which was published a few days after our video interview. Both text and project raised a healthy amount of critical response, generally favourable. However, a number of computer scientists and art critics expressed their concerns, mostly on Twitter, in relation to Crawford and Paglen's stand on the importance of preserving training sets, the confusions that can emerge when datasets with very different histories and logics are exhibited together, and Paglen's selection and display choices on the occasion of his later commission at the Barbican Curve in London.

This noise was welcomed, considering the urgency of the issues at stake, which call into question wider dynamics of data governance, copyright, privacy and surveillance. In a sense, it acted as a reminder that we – as users, spectators, researchers, art practitioners and citizens who live in the privileged side of the digital "divide" – need to maintain a degree of critical alertness when it comes to assessing the politics of representation in the algorithmic world. Primarily, because we are both the objects and subjects of this cycle of spectacle-extraction-spectacle. This is a key consideration that should inform the way in which datasets are presented to the wider public through the programming of cultural organisations, where critical reflections on users' agency and human-machine visual literacy can be raised.

From this perspective, *Training Humans* proved to be important not so much for the individual images

---

6   Crawford, K. and Paglen, T. (2019) 'The Politics of Images in Machine Learning Training Sets.' Available at: https://excavating.ai (Accessed 10 February 2021).

it displayed – which the neurons in the visual cortex processed as easily as they forgot – but for the critical debate it staged around the wider implications of seemingly innocuous practices of image making and image sharing. These problems do not require a binary conversation, nor one conducted by a 'few key players' only. Rather, it needs to be a much more nuanced and collective one. We ought to use our human intelligence, together with that of our machines, to pay attention to the granular as well as to the systemic, to the materiality of images as well as their invisible networks of power and circulation. In other words, we need to keep questioning what we see, but also what we do not see; what is being said and what is not being said, by whom and in which context. After all, vision, as the founder of ImageNet Fei-Fei Li reminds us, "begins with the eyes but truly starts with the brain".[7]

---

7   Fei-Fei, L. (2015) *How we're teaching computers to understand pictures,* Ted Talk, 23 March 2015. Available at: https://www.ted.com/talks/fei_fei_li_how_we_re_teaching_computers_to_understand_pictures?language=se (Accessed 10 February 2021).

To Look Like a Dataset; revisiting the Data/Set/Match project

Nicolas Malevé

At the bottom of a black screen, a caption reads: "Acrobatics, tumbling. The gymnastic moves of an acrobat." Then, abruptly, a batch of 400 photographs are displayed on the screen sequentially at a speed that defies human perception. To a certain degree, the text on the screen helps to grasp the content of these images. Flashy tops; upside down figures; intricate choreographies of bodies in mid-air, on the ground, in a circus-like atmosphere, in exterior settings or inside a house. Batons, hoops, bicycles, pommel horses, balloons punctuate the rapid visual flow. After a while a second black screen announces a new cycle. This time, the animation moves to the category "track and field, participating in athletic sports performed on a running track." Athletes running, passing over hurdles or throwing javelins, succeed the acrobats of the previous sequence. A jumble of jersey numbers, track markings, arms, legs and running shoes. During this seemingly infinite flow, the animation is randomly paused and an image is displayed full screen for two seconds. An image sample is arbitrarily given more time. This image does not illustrate the definition better than any other. It is not more aesthetically compelling and sometimes, even, its poor resolution makes it barely legible. These halts are too short to give the viewer the time to scrutinise the details of the visual surface. However, as the animation moves from athletes to microbes, from flowers to forests, from dishwashers to criminals, a random halt is enough to get a sense of the provenance of the photographs: news photos, family snapshots, laboratory samples, submarine photographs, newspaper scans, webcam stills, screenshots or memes. These photographs extracted from every corner of the web, optimised for circulation, are now distributed into categories.

The animation *Exhibiting ImageNet* is displayed on an eight panel screen – the Media Wall of The Photographers' Gallery – visible from the street with high impact for visitors entering the building, on their way to the cafeteria, the bookshop, or taking the elevator to the exhibition floors. If they have the curiosity, they can watch a live broadcast of the animation on YouTube running around the clock, even when the institution is closed. The animation continues at pace with random interruptions through photos of items as diverse as queen consorts, salesmen, Appaloosas, prairie dogs, honeycreepers, fighting cocks, Greco-Roman wrestlers. It seems that there is space for every creature crawling, jumping, running, swimming or sleeping and for every living or non-living thing, object, machine, instrument, device. Everything that has a steering wheel, handlebars, a doorknob, a handle, a stick, a neck or a grip. Microbes, diseases, infections as well as weddings, birthday parties and Christmas celebrations are treated equally: a few milliseconds of screen time. However, in this never-ending catalogue of photographs of everything, there is an absent category: the category *photograph* itself.

Exhibiting ImageNet displays the 14 million photos of the ImageNet dataset: one of the most renowned collections of photographs that computer scientists use to train machine vision algorithms.[1] The scale of this dataset signals the significant role photography plays in computer vision. Yet the notable absence of the photograph as a category in this all-encompassing database suggests that the relation between machine vision and the medium it feeds off remains unclear.

Exhibiting ImageNet functioned as the public introduction to Data/Set/Match; a year-long programme seeking new ways to present, visualise and interrogate contemporary image datasets. This essay, written while editing the present book, revisits the project, the research and the questions that led to it and asks how it can induce new beginnings and not just concluding remarks. What can we learn from the research that lay behind the work and how does it relate to the specific context in which it was conducted?

The circuit of vision

Data/Set/Match is built upon previous research and artistic work that engaged with the techno-cultural formation of photography as part of The Photographers' Gallery Digital Programme. Since the early days of the programme, the framework of the networked image has been a key concept to approach the problem of curating and exhibiting digital photography. As Katrina Sluis explains in her conversation with Ioanna Zouli in this book [see pp.7-28], the programme initially concentrated on questions of cultural value in-

1   Deng, J., Dong, W., Socher, R., Li, L., Li, K. and Fei-Fei, L. (2009) 'Imagenet: A large-scale hierarchical image database' DOI.: 10.1109/ CVPR.2009.5206848.

creasingly shared and circulated amongst the various communities forming around digital images. The networked image is more than an image travelling across communication networks. It is an image that functions within the separate registers of visuality and computer code.[2] The relation between these registers is opaque and power laden. Addressing the computational dimension of the networked image demands a new set of conceptual tools and methods. As Sluis remarks, these tools and methods are even more necessary as contemporary mechanisms of power, embedded in the visual, cannot be understood only through looking at relations between humans mediated by images. The place of a larger computational apparatus in these power relations needs to be found.

Essentially, Data/Set/Match began with a preliminary mapping of the "circuit of vision.[3]" The circuit of vision – a term coined by the independent researcher Jara Rocha – consists in the relational cartography of all the actors, human and non-human, taking part in the production, maintenance and circulation of ma-

---

2   For a detailed discussion of the networked image, see: Rubinstein, D. and Sluis, K. (2008) 'A LIFE MORE PHOTOGRAPHIC', *Photographies*, 1 (1), pp. 9-28. DOI:10.1080/17540760701785842; Dewdney, A. (2018) 'Co-creating in the Networks.' Available at: https://thephotographersgallery.org.uk/viewpoints/2/co-creating-networks (Accessed 28 February 2019); Tedone, G. (2019) 'Curating The Networked Image: Circulation, Commodification, Computation', PhD thesis, London South Bank University, London; Centre for the Study of the Networked Image, Cox, G., Dekker, A., Dewdney, A. and Sluis, K. (2021) 'Affordances of the Networked Image', *The Nordic Journal of Aesthetics* 30 (61-62 SE-Articles), pp. 40-45. https://tidsskrift.dk/nja/article/view/127857 (Accessed 24 January 2022).

3   The researcher and artist Jara Rocha uses the expression "circuit of vision" in her work and teaching to emphasise the relevance of the many invisibilised actors in the production of machine vision.

chine vision. Machine vision is not treated here as a black box but as a complex circuit where every agent "works" and contributes to the learning and performance of algorithms, as Jon Uriarte explains in detail in *Working with Datasets* [see pp.39-43]. In this cartography, we identify the dataset as an obligatory passage point.[4] Following the circuit of vision does not merely imply introducing different objects. It invites an emphasis upon the relational texture of photography. When machine vision is considered as a circuit, every juncture, every connection in the circuit is an entry point for enquiry and for interventions that may affect its programmability. Understanding machine vision as a circuit opens up a diverse field of practice. The dataset finds its significance when we recognise the entanglement of photography and technology, and the chain of actors involved in their relation.

It is crucial to complement the notion of circuit with another notion that gives it dimensionality: scale. The rationale for creating large datasets is the hypothesis that algorithms trained with more data are better equipped to cope with a variety of visual forms when they operate in unconstrained environments.[5] With more data, computer scientists consider that algorithms will be able to learn from the myriad of differences of the image world. With current machine learn-

4   Jaton, F. (2017) 'We get the algorithms of our ground truths: Designing referential databases in digital image processing', *Social Studies of Science*, 47 (6), pp. 811-840. DOI:10.1177/0306312717730428.

5   State-of-the-art algorithms such as Facebook's DeepFace or Google's FaceNet are trained with millions of images. Hu G., Peng X., Yang Y., Hospedales T. and Verbeek J. (2016), 'Frankenstein: Learning Deep Face Representations Using Small Data', in: *Computing Research Repository*, http://arxiv.org/abs/1603.06470 (Accessed 4 November 2020).

ing techniques, there is a growing consensus among practitioners that increasing availability of sample data may provoke a qualitative change in the algorithm's performance. At this stage, it is worth recapitulating the consequences of working at a new scale. To do so, I will use the example of ImageNet, the 14-million-photographs dataset I briefly introduced above.

Datasets like ImageNet depend on the availability of large volumes of photos. Each category of ImageNet reportedly contains a minimum of 1000 images and its categories include a vast variety of topics from plants and geological formations to people and animals. To acquire the quantity of needed images, computer scientists turn to the internet, a "treasure trove of images"[6] where photos are downloaded *en masse* without notifying photographers nor attempting to obtain consent from the parties represented in them. In his contribution to the present volume, Alan Blackwell [see pp. 117-129] discusses how the inherent extractivism of this mode of acquisition of visual data turns the creative labour of countless photographers into a repository of human intelligence available for mining.

If the production of a dataset begins with the acquisition of data, the work of annotation that follows (tagging, classifying, filtering duplicates or irrelevant data) is at least as impressive as the number of photographs amassed by engineers. The work of manually cross-referencing and labelling the photos is what makes datasets like ImageNet so unique. The automation of vision has not reduced but rather increased the

6   GoogleTechTalks (2011) 'Large-scale Image Classification: ImageNet and ObjectBank.' Available at: https://www.youtube.com/watch?v=qd DHp29QVdw (Accessed 28 February 2021).

number of eyeballs looking at images, of hands typing descriptions, of taggers and annotators. It has created a new context in which the activity of seeing is taking place, where retinas are entangled in heavily technical environments. In these environments, repetitive tasks test the physical resistance of the people performing them[7] and, for annotators, the ability to embody scale is a condition for survival.

Crowdsourcing platforms such as Amazon Mechanical Turk (AMT) are used to recruit workers who classify images under precarious labour conditions. Machine vision would not exist in its current form without the mediation of different platforms providing free or cheap labour. Without Flickr, ImageNet would not have been able to collect photographs at scale. Without AMT, it would not have been able to mobilise the large workforce needed to annotate billions of images. Annotation is cognitive labour. To annotate is the activity that consists of the articulation of the dual register of the photograph: to bridge the gap between the photograph as a visual surface and the photograph as data. To bridge this gap is a labour-intensive activity. For this reason, I will use the expression "photographic elaboration" to refer to the process of visual data processing performed through crowdsourcing platforms.[8]

Engaged in the process of photographic elaboration, annotators are not passive viewers. They interpret, filter, and clean thousands of images, and they have to ac-

7   Irani, L. C. (2015) 'The cultural work of microwork', *New Media & Society*, 17 (5), pp. 720-739. DOI: http://dx.doi.org/10.1177/1461444813511926.

8   For a development of the concept of photographic elaboration see Malevé, N. (2020) 'On the Data Set's Ruins', *AI & SOCIETY*. DOI: https://doi.org/10.1007/s00146-020-01093-w.

complish these tasks in the blink of an eye. To produce a dataset at "the scale of the web" imposes a particular way of seeing images. The interfaces of AMT are designed to guide workers. Their vision is oriented and framed. Their work is divided into micro tasks and, if they want to make a living from their labour, they need to function at a pace that barely allows them to see the images. From this perspective, a speed of vision is built economically into the platform. For the annotators, structurally, the glance is the norm, not the gaze. The speed also corresponds to the ever-increasing demand from the software industry for training sets that can be produced fast: legions of workers are mobilised intensely for short periods of time. Through the interfaces of AMT, the employers of the annotators manage the cadence of the annotation work. As the volume of requests increases, the unit of measurement for a labelling task moves towards the millisecond rather than the second.

Further, the scale of dataset production encompasses a geopolitical dimension. Workers, in the words of Florian Schmidt, "have to navigate highly complex, volatile and opaque global markets for the production of ground truth data" [see pp.65-73]. Supranational corporations outsource the work of annotation to countries of the Global South in a vertiginous chain of intermediaries where clients and subcontractors are unknown to each other. This produces a circuit built on a mutual unawareness of employers and workers and a striking opacity regarding the reach and depth of the network of intermediaries that connects them.

Finally, mapping the circuit of vision and sizing its scale shows the ambiguous role computer scientists give to the photograph, the category so notoriously absent in

ImageNet. Mapping the circuit of vision highlights the fact that dataset production relies heavily on the supposed transparency of the photo. Photographs can be parsed in a glance by workers in a hurry. In the annotation environment, photographs are both crucial and taken for granted. A huge assemblage of machines and humans is needed to hold them in place, to acquire them from all corners of the internet and to pair them with labels. This process is driven by a confidence in the diaphaneity of photographs. Photography is the site where what we see and what we know can be reconciled: cats, dogs and microwaves coincide neatly with their representations in gifs and jpegs. However, as Geoff Cox [see pp.31-37] building on John Berger's essay *Ways of Seeing* reminds us, the relation between what we see and what we know is never settled. Looking at the photographic elaboration of computer vision, we realise that annotation is not simply an affair of seeing through representations. It is acquiring content, embodying a scale, negotiating speed, adjusting to micro-work and navigating volatile markets. The relation of things seen and things known cannot be settled because their unresolved relation is inseparable from the controversies, labour conflicts, epistemic divergences thriving all along the circuit of vision. This brings the problem for the practitioners involved in the Digital Programme: how to engage with such a circuit, its tensions, its problems of representation, its scales and speeds? And how to do that in the context of a photography institution such as The Photographers' Gallery?

<u>Exhibiting the dataset,
inhabiting its scale</u>

The practices reflected in this book and on *Unthinking Photography*[9] online go beyond a critique of computer vision. They are also speculative and exploratory. The engagement of the practitioners who contributed to Data/Set/Match has taken different directions. They have investigated the process of annotation with a high degree of precision. They have engaged with the dataset as a structure and a form, with its politics of classification and its condition of labour. In this sense, they don't take the dataset as a readily legible object. They have asked what a dataset is, but more importantly what it can be and which kind of world it enacts. The practitioners in Data/Set/Match pursue a direction that contrasts with the attempts by the computer vision community to remedy its problems and prevent risk. They embrace the complexity of the dataset as a techno-cultural object. Here the problem is not to contain its potential for harm, but to explore the potential that is excluded by the practices of computer science. They are engaged in a process of defamiliarisation. Their starting point is to resist the reduction of the dataset to a statistical distribution of objects with measurable attributes. The dataset becomes an object with more facets, a field of multiple resonances. One whose existence within culture and science needs to be interrogated anew.

9   A significant part of the research material accompanying Data/Set/
     Match has been published on the Unthinking Photography platform
     during the development of the project.

See IMG 14 on page 189

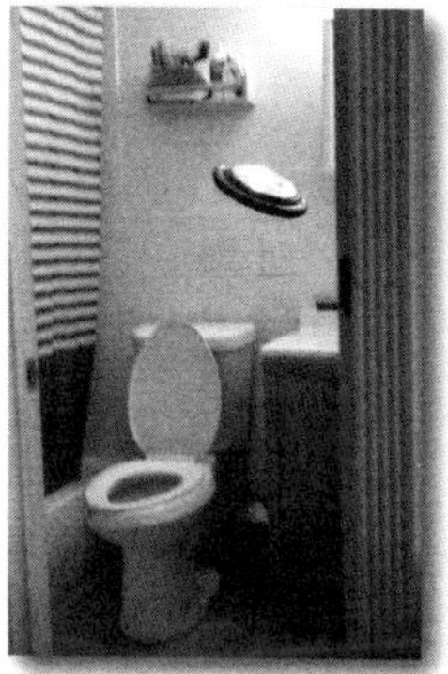

'toilet, sink, frisbee', 35mm B/W film. Part
of the Tunnel Vision (2020) project by Philipp Schmitt.

Philipp Schmitt's *Tunnel Vision*[10] offers an example of
a practice that extends the boundaries of the dataset.
Tunnel Vision is a work that confronts the notion of
context that undergirds the *COCO* (*Common Objects
in Context*) dataset. In his work, Schmitt plays with the
rules of formation of the dataset and the logics it enacts.
The COCO dataset was created with the goal of advanc-
ing the state-of-the-art in object recognition and scene
understanding. This has been achieved by "gathering
images of complex everyday scenes containing common
objects in their natural context".[11] Schmitt explains that

10   Schmitt, P. (2020) 'Tunnel Vision', *Unthinking Photography*. Available
      at: https://unthinking.photography/articles/tunnel-vision (Accessed 23
      August 2021).

11   Lin, T.-Y., Maire, M., Belongie, S., Bourdev, L., Girshick, R., Hays, J.,
      et al. (2015) 'Microsoft COCO: Common Objects in Context.' Fleet,
      D., Pajdla, T., Schiele, B., Tuytelaars, T. (eds) Computer Vision – ECCV
      2014. ECCV 2014. Lecture Notes in Computer Science, vol 8693.
      Springer, Cham. https://doi.org/10.1007/978-3-319-10602-1_48.

researchers acquired the dataset photos by combining different object categories as search terms. For instance, they scoured Flickr for images corresponding to combinations of terms such as "person + bicycle" or "pizza + dining table." The co-occurrence of two terms is treated as a "context" in COCO's world. Schmitt approaches COCO as a combinatorial space. His objective is to take the procedural logic of the dataset to its limit. By doing so, he explores the inherent weirdness of COCO. Schmitt exhausts the potential co-occurrences in the dataset and extrapolates the "common contexts" they suggest. If the co-occurrence of "person" and "bicycle" creates a context that evokes a familiar scene, what to make of a context where "pizza" meets "fire hydrant" or where "cat" meets "sink"? To ask these questions, the artist scans the dataset for such co-occurrences and selects the images where these unlikely "contexts" occur. In this process, the experience of looking "resembles a form of algorithmic tunnel vision where peripheral details are blacked out and nothing but COCO objects come into focus". Schmitt even goes a step further and takes his camera to the streets, where he looks for such unlikely encounters in his surroundings. In his project, the problem is less an ethics of representation than an ethics of defamiliarisation. It raises the question of the definition of a common context and the tunnel vision it entails. The object of Schmitt's work is the formal solution adopted by the COCO researchers. To treat a co-occurrence between two terms as a context means to embed a procedural logic in the dataset. Schmitt looks for ways to probe what this logic makes us see and how it makes us relate to the world. Schmitt's problems with COCO are not the representations the dataset contains, what one sees *in* the dataset. More importantly, it is the problem of what it means to look *like* a dataset.

Transitioning from the question of looking at the dataset to the question of looking like one also requires addressing the dataset as a scale and a speed. As I observed earlier, dataset annotators barely have the time to look at the photographs they classify. The dataset, an object which defines so much of what machines "see", is only glanced upon. What is the nature of what can be perceived by the annotators in a few hundred milliseconds? What is emphasised, what is overlooked and how is the complexity of the photographic object dealt with? How can we engage with the dataset as more than a provider of representation, but as a flow of kinetic energy where those who were annotating the dataset barely had the time to blink and glance? Texts by the artists in this book give some idea of what it entails to develop a visual intimacy with such large objects. The analysis of Everest Pipkin, in particular, emphasises the importance of learning how to attune rhythmically with the dataset. "I learn the exact length of 3 seconds" writes Pipkin [see pp.105-115]. To engage with the dataset is a visual task embedded in a very specific temporality where long hours of work are divided into micro-temporal sequences.

In the same vein, the key motivation for the *Exhibiting ImageNet* project that introduced this essay was to make the viewer experience the temporal scale inherent to the work of annotation. One key issue about ImageNet is the sheer difficulty to comprehend, physically locate and even "see" it. When I created the Exhibiting ImageNet display, I worked with the Digital Programme team to develop a script that cycled through ImageNet at a speed of 90 milliseconds per image, traversing the entire dataset in a period of two months. The script paused at random points to enable the viewer to take some of the images in. By doing so, the project aimed to raise questions about the relation of scale between the overwhelming quantities of images needed to train algorithms and the human attention required to make sense of this flow of data. It applied linearly the formula Fei-Fei Li used to calculate the time it would take to create the total number of ImageNet's annotations. This formula can be expressed in the following terms:[12]

— given a total of 40,000 categories
— multiplied by 1,000 images per category
— multiplied by the number of annotators
agreeing on the result
— the time to completion is estimated
at 600,000,000 seconds or 19 years
— at the expressed condition that the annotator
only spends 200 miliseconds in front of each image.

This obviously exceeds the ability of one individual, who would have to stay awake for 19 years, blinking only when necessary without missing one or more images, and avoiding any distraction. In *Exhibiting ImageNet*, this logic is pushed to its extreme. The script on display "blinks" every 90 milliseconds to take in the image briefly appearing on screen. It compresses 19 years into two months. It is ImageNet's ideal viewer. By enacting

12   Fei-Fei, L. (2010) 'ImageNet, crowdsourcing, benchmarking & other cool things', in: *CMU VASC Seminar.*

this ideal viewer, my goal was to address the dataset as a scale that enables a certain optics through which an infrastructure of sight becomes palpable.

What these projects help us understand is the importance of considering datasets as more than collections of visual samples closed upon themselves, and instead as seeing devices in their own right. The work carried out during Data/Set/Match also shows that the exponential development of datasets signals more than a change in the supply chain of computer vision. It transforms how machines learn to see. This in turn impacts the ways in which humans are learning to see. Machines and annotators alike are learning to see like a dataset; a fact that raises the stakes when negotiating the terms of this mutual learning. If there is a "common context" to be found in machine vision, it should not be sought in the accidental co-occurrences of labels but in the common experience of seeing mediated by the dataset.

A digital programme in the photographic institution

To work with datasets opens up a space for learning that goes beyond the individual objects that are selected in the datasets. What is less apparent to those who visited the Gallery and participated in the Data/Set/Match events is that working with datasets has also been an occasion to learn about the institution in which the project took place. Inhabiting the scales and circuits of computer vision affected the Gallery. Generally, the projects shown during Data/Set/Match challenged the technical infrastructure of the institution. In particular, producing an animation such as *Exhib-*

iting ImageNet forced all the parties involved to gain a deeper understanding of the material infrastructure of the gallery. Performing at a scale of 14 million images is a straining process. The curatorial team became intimately and materially engaged with the dataset through its attachments and relays: platforms such as Flickr, archive.org; a host of human agents (from helpful archivists to angry sys-admins); high bandwidth and fragile cables; the unpredictability of browser caches and the importance of floating-point numbers. The constant failures and fixes that were necessary to maintain the project provides an insight into the instability and frequent movement of this infrastructure. But, more importantly, it begs questions about the assumptions built into the technical and material infrastructure of the institution itself.

Digital technology permeates the whole institution. Email correspondence with artists, curators and art dealers; flight bookings; Instagram posts from the cafeteria customers; documents sent by the staff to the shared printer; website updates, all circulate through the same network but with different partitions and privileges. The traffic of all these elements is handled by the same passage point: the institution's router. They are all translated digitally, yet they are not all understood as the "digital" among the members of the institution. As Andrew Dewdney[13] and Ioanna Zouli[14]

13   Dewdney, A. (2019) 'The Networked Image: The Flight Of Cultural Authority And The Multiple Times And Spaces Of The Art Museum', in: Lewi, H., Smith, W., Cooke, S., and vom Lehn, D. (eds.) *The Routledge International Handbook in New Digital Practices in Galleries, Libraries Archives, Museums and Heritage Sites*. New York: Routledge.

14   Zouli, I. (2018) *Digital Tate: the use of video and the construction of audiences*. PhD thesis. London South Bank University, London.

demonstrated in their respective analyses of the technology at Tate, attention must be paid to the different understandings of the "digital" within a single art institution. At The Photographers' Gallery, the so-called digital technology can be found everywhere inside the institution's walls, yet only a strand of the programme officially deals with "the" digital, and this is the Digital Programme. In the institution, the "digital" functions in a dual mode. In the first sense, it is treated as a resource. Here, the term digital refers to a technology that supports the functioning of the institution. It concerns the administrative work or the communication handled by the press and marketing departments. In the second sense, it is treated as a curatorial object. In a circumscribed partition of the institution, a "digital" project does not only refer to a format but to a complex configuration of practices, institutional territories, practitioners and kinds of display. What the intensity of the project lays bare is the difficulty to rely on the same infrastructure for both. By transmitting 14 million images over two months, the gallery gets attuned to the rhythms and scales of the formation of machine learning and not just the consumption of its products. To cope with the constant movement of data, it needs to redeploy its network: to reach out for other connections, stabilise its relations, monitor the flows of incoming and outgoing data. There is a constant difficulty in keeping up with the scale of the traffic and remaining synchronised with external servers. With Data/Set/Match, the infrastructure of the institution hits its limit.

The technical infrastructure of the institution is display-oriented. It embeds the idea that a display of visuals is expected rather than a technological engagement with a network of operation. We hit the limit of the distribution of the digital as resource and theme. To attune with the scale and rhythms of dataset annotation, we are touching its material contours. To extend this limit, however, means more than purchasing more web space or upgrading a technical network. The question raised here cannot be reduced to a mere practical problem. The constant tension suffered by the infrastructure tells us something about the position of the institution regarding technology: it is configured to be at the receiving end of technology. However, the different texts in this publication and the various projects in the Data/Set/Match programme point towards another direction. What would it mean for the institution to consider itself as an entry point in the formation of technology?

<u>The institution and its relations:
entering the community of vision</u>

During the conference organised at The Photographers' Gallery on the occasion of the 10th birthday of ImageNet, Fei-Fei Li acknowledged that the problems posed by computer vision could not be resolved by the computer science community alone.[15] Now that computer vision operates "in the wild", there is a need for interdisciplinary collaboration to tackle the problems that, in part, it created and, in part, exacerbated. The *vision community*, as machine vision scientists name a gather-

---

15   Fei-Fei, L. (2020) 'Where Did ImageNet Come From?' Available at: https://unthinking.photography/articles/where-did-imagenet-come-from (Accessed 19 March 2021).

ing of researchers from optics, signal theory, computer science and cognitive psychology,[16] has been unable to cope with the ever-increasing challenges faced by technologists. As many of the articles in this book and elsewhere[17] have pointed out, the use of computer vision has contributed to various documented instances of racial or sexual discrimination and helped reproduce systemic imbalances. Data/Set/Match has highlighted the importance of opening computer vision to other forms of knowledge production that involve artists, activists and the public of cultural institutions. At this juncture, it is worth reflecting on the potential for questioning and engaging with machine vision in the specific context of a photographic institution.

Along with the project comes an invitation to the institution to adopt a certain role. The Gallery's long interaction with photography makes it a candidate of choice to force the discussion about the photographic elaboration of computer vision. It has a cultural standing that can, in some measure, counterbalance the authority of the engineering community over its products. Its status as a long-standing institution could be used as leverage to provoke an opening in the vision community to a larger set of actors. Throughout the

16 Fei-Fei, L. (2012) 'Computers that see'. Available at: https://www.you tube.com/watch?v=viwpTTvSQKM (Accessed 2 January 2021).

17 See in particular Buolamwini, J. and Gebru, T. (2018) 'Gender Shades: Intersectional Accuracy Disparities in Commercial Gender Classification', in: Friedler, S. A. and Wilson, C. (eds.) *Proceedings of the 1st Conference on Fairness, Accountability and Transparency.* New York, NY, USA: PMLR, 81, pp. 77-91; and Bender, E. M., Gebru, T., McMillan-Major, A. and Shmitchell, S. (2021) 'On the Dangers of Stochastic Parrots: Can Language Models Be Too Big?', in: *Proceedings of the 2021 ACM Conference on Fairness, Accountability, and Transparency.* New York, NY, USA: Association for Computing Machinery, pp. 610-623.

project, the Digital Programme set the stage for an active and concrete collaboration. It outlined the nature of the relevant knowledge an institution can help produce. The question that comes up now is: will the institution, building on the work accomplished in the Digital Programme, claim its membership to the vision community? And, insisting on the importance of the photographic elaboration of computer vision, can it reclaim computer vision as a photographic project?

This can be achieved on condition that the institution takes on an expansive understanding of its role. As I noted, in ImageNet the category "photograph" is notoriously absent, whilst photographs are the sites where dataset creators hope to reconcile things and their representations. The role of the photographic institution is to problematise what it means to look like a dataset and to engage with the political tensions, the scales, the rhythms, the misrepresentations and the epistemic instabilities that the vision community shies away from. To do that, it must not conceive of its role exclusively in terms of being an art institution, an authority on the artfulness of the medium, an arbiter of photographic professionalism, and a protector of such standards as good photography. It must instead act as a platform where the various alignments of practices, devices and ways of seeing coming and going under the name "photography" can be explored in their active role in the modelling of the technologies of vision. It must conceive of its place not at the receiving end of technology but in its formation. It must stand for photography not only as image, but more importantly as a set of practices and processes informing how vision is enacted through technology.

Challenge for the
photographic institution

At this point it is worth taking note of Gaia Tedone's commentary on the limitations of the white cube and the gallery [see pp.131-139]. Reflecting on the show *Training Humans* by Crawford and Paglen, Tedone asks: how can a critical engagement with machine vision go further than the spectacle of critique? The same question also has to be asked of the Data/Set/Match project. How, in the context of cultural hyperproduction, can the institution invest in a long-term commitment to effectuate change, rather than turn the page and move on to the next exhibition? These are difficult questions for institutions of photography that are hard pressed to generate audience ratings, public footfall and attention. Beyond the ethical questions regarding the inclusion of datasets in exhibitions, Tedone's question addresses the institutional politics involved in such exhibitions. How does exhibiting the dataset engage the institution in new networks of solidarity and processes of transformation? How does this affect the institution's responsibilities for future exhibitions and activities?

The answer to these questions lies in thinking about long-term commitment, which is why this reflexive and prospective reading of the Data/Set/Match project is necessary. I began this discussion of the role of the institution by considering its technical configuration and I said that it implied a certain position towards technology. This question is bound to larger institutional questions. What position can a photographic institution occupy regarding the vision community? Which kind of alliances does it require? How can it sustain this position over time? The problems and questions raised in this book and the practices that informed it require active engagement as well as outreach. Racism, sexism or exploitation are not mere problems of bias stemming from bad representations that can be locally resolved in the datasets. Continuing the work initiated in this project implies developing ties with artists, educationalists, trade unionists, activists, developers and researchers committed to fighting against discrimination and racism.

The limits of the peer review model of computer vision have been exposed crudely to the public in recent years. Datasets have been at the centre of controversies that have given rise to public scrutiny and outcry. The various critiques aimed at ImageNet have been amply debated in the press. But ImageNet is only one example of the many datasets wherein bias has been exposed, and many of these datasets have simply been moved offline as a consequence. However, what is particularly worrying about ImageNet is how it gained such an honorific status within the computer science community while being plagued with such glaring problems. How can the recipient of the prestigious PAMI Longuet-Higgins Prize[18] classify *Transexual* below *Anomaly, Unusual Person* and next to *Aberrant, Zombie* or *Ugly Duckling*?[19] How can one of the highest cited papers of the discipline appropriate images without referring

18   The Longuet-Higgins Prize recognises computer vision papers from ten years ago for their significant impact on the field. See: The Computer Vision Foundation (2020) Computer Vision Awards. Available at: https://www.thecvf.com/?page_id=413#LHP (Accessed 23 June 2021).

19   For a more extensive discussion of ImageNet's classification problem, see Crawford, K. and Paglen, T. (2019) 'Excavating AI. The Politics of Images in Machine Learning Training Sets'. Available at: https://www.excavating.ai/ (Accessed 19 March 2021).

to their authors, include people's portraits without permission, and recycle racist, homophobic and misogynistic imagery?

The corrective actions proposed by various groups of computer scientists are obviously necessary. Current attempts to de-bias the dataset, to increase dataset traceability or to increase the diversity of programming teams are more than welcome. However, these issues are systemic. There is a need to connect struggles against racial discrimination, homophobia and the general toxicity present at all the articulations of the circuit of vision, as well as to support and relay the work of those who resist technological forms of dominance. Commitment in the long term is of the essence as these alliances require trust to be built over time. Were it to end now without thinking about its re-introduction, without thinking about how it engages the institution and its conditions of effectuating change, Data/Set/Match would end up in what Tedone calls "spectacle" – a display of criticality that replaces engagement. Curation of artworks and exhibitions alone is not enough. They need to connect and extend networks of collectives and institutions aimed at effectuating change.

Work in progress

More than the contents of the datasets, Data/Set/Match questioned the mode of knowledge production of computer vision and how it defines what counts as knowledge. It is important here to insist on the issue at stake when discussing the role of The Photographers' Gallery: to provide a context where computer vision's mode of knowledge production, the effects of epistemic boundaries and exclusions can be probed. To provide a context where its objects can be rediscovered anew. It supported a research project whose premise is that computer vision has been a techno-cultural project all along.

The fact that the institution dedicated time and financial support to develop activities around and a reflection of the relation between technology and photography needs to be highlighted and appreciated. In turn, it is equally important to acknowledge that this project could exist because the institution did not merely curate photography projects but contributed to the development of networks of knowledge creation. Data/Set/Match was an alliance between an institution of higher learning, the Centre of the Study of the Networked Image at London South Bank University,[20] and The Photographers' Gallery, who continue to work together. The relation between the two opens the possibility of research carried out over a time period that differs from the quick pace of an art institution submitted to the imperatives of cultural programming. While the research develops, issues have the time to mature and prepare the ground for an item of programming such as an exhibition or a conference. It introduces a dialogue between different modalities and temporalities. This particular articulation between academic research, intervention in situ and public events has been a condition for the research process to develop in a way that draws from the resources of the academy and unfolds in public at the same time. This alliance served as a structure to connect with many other actors. Over the years, many organisations and collectives have contributed to the

---

20   See https://www.centreforthestudyof.net/ (Accessed 24 June 2021).

research and creation of the Digital Programme, such as Animate Projects, Brighton Photo Biennial, Fotomuseum Winterthur, University of Sussex, Westminster University, University of Exeter, University of the Arts London, Arts Council England, Lucerne University of Applied Sciences and Arts, Foto Colectania in Barcelona, London Alternative Photography Collective, Hemera Collective, South Bank Collective, Geocities Research Institute, Scandinavian Institute of Computational Vandalism, to name a few.

The existence of such an inter-institutional construction and its network of collaborators is instrumental in having a chance to interrogate and imagine a horizon of change for computer vision in a context that does not preemptively foreclose modes of inquiry foreign to computer science. It is of particular importance now as a massive influx of governmental and industry money supports an AI curriculum designed exclusively according to the disciplinary principles of computer scientists.[21] It is crucial to underline the relevance of the contributions coming from networks of knowledge production such as the collaboration between The Photographers' Gallery and the Centre of the Study of the Networked Image since 2012. Any inquiry into the photographic elaboration of computer vision that is deemed either irrelevant or actively discouraged in the disciplinary pre-

---

21   A good example in the UK is the aforementioned AI Sector Deal based on a report written by Regius Professor of Computer at the University of Southampton. Dame Wendy Hall and Meta's Vice President of AI, Jérôme Pesenti. As an outcome of the deal, the government committed to invest £406 million in "maths, digital and technical education, helping to address the shortage of science, technology, engineering and maths (STEM) skills" Gov.uk (2017) 'AI Sector Deal'. Available at: https://www.gov.uk/government/publications/artificial-intelligence-sector-deal/ai-sector-deal (Accessed 24 June 2021).

cincts of machine vision needs an alternative network of actors and institutions that support such research questions. The very existence of the Data/Set/Match project shows how the consolidation of such partnerships is the pre-condition for critical questions to be asked about the experimental formation of machine vision, its scales and its photographic elaboration.

When the time comes to revisit a project, it is necessary to underscore how the projects and the institutional alliances come together. A dataset can be approached as a complex object only in a context that makes room for its complexity. To learn to see like a dataset can be dehumanising, as the annotators on crowdsourcing platforms might attest. As the writings in this publication demonstrate, it can also be a process of learning where human and non-human ways of seeing can be negotiated. This requires the collaboration of artists, cultural producers, activists, educationalists, thinkers, critical technologists and speculative hackers. Crucially, it also requires an institutional backbone. In this sense, the creation of speculative technologies and divergent datasets is a work in progress, and so is the development of the institutional backbone they rely on.

Thanks to Andrew Dewdney, Katrina Sluis and Laurence Rassel for their valuable feedback.

Katrina Sluis

is Head of Photography & Media Arts in the School of Art & Design at The Australian National University, Canberra. Prior to joining ANU, Katrina was based in London where she was Senior Lecturer and founding Co-Director of the Centre for the Study of the Networked Image (CSNI), London South Bank University. From 2011-19 she also held the inaugural post of Senior Curator (Digital Programmes) at The Photographers' Gallery, London developing artistic commissions and public projects on machine vision, synthetic imaging, net culture and speculative photographic education. She is the co-editor of the book, *The Networked Image in Post-Digital Culture* (Routledge).

Ioanna Zouli

is a researcher and curator. She writes, translates, and teaches on network culture, museums and visual practices online. She has worked with organisations in the UK and Greece, including The Photographers' Gallery, Tate, the Royal College of Art, the Onassis Foundation and Ethnofest. She was a curatorial fellow of the Stavros Niarchos Foundation 'Artworks Fellowship Program' and Writer-in-Residence at Onassis AiR - School of Infinite Rehearsals: Movement III. She is the commissioning editor of *Unthinking Photography* since 2016 and a research associate at the Centre for the Study of the Networked Image (CSNI) at London South Bank University as well as the Centre of New Media and Feminist Public Practices at the University of Thessaly, Greece.

Geoff Cox

is Associate Professor/co-Director of the Centre for the Study of the Networked Image (CSNI) at London South Bank University (UK) and Adjunct Associate Professor at Aarhus University (DK), where he has been engaged (with Jacob Lund) on a research project *The Contemporary Condition* funded by the Danish Council for Independent Research. As part of this, he published *The Contemporary Condition: Introductory Thoughts on Contemporaneity and Contemporary Art* (with Jacob Lund) as the first in a series of small co-edited books published by Sternberg Press (2016). He co-runs a yearly workshop/publication in collaboration with transmediale festival in Berlin (since 2012) and is co-editor of the associated open access online journal APRJA (with Christian Ulrik Andersen), as well as editor for the open access DATA browser book series (Open Humanities Press, with Joasia Krysa). He has a research interest in software studies and contemporary aesthetics, expressed in occasional artworks and numerous publications including *Speaking Code* (MIT Press 2013; with Alex McLean), and *Aesthetic Programming* (Open Humanities Press 2020; with Winnie Soon). Amongst other things he is currently working on a multi-authored book project about live coding (with Alan Blackwell, Emma Cocker, Thor Magnusson, Alex McLean), and an ongoing research project entitled *Ways of Machine Seeing.*

Jon Uriarte

is an artist, educator and curator. Jon is curator of Digital Programme at The Photographers' Gallery in London, UK, and curator of Getxophoto Image Festival in Getxo, Spain. He previously curated DONE, a programme on the impact of digital technologies and the internet on the contemporary image landscape launched by Foto Colectania in Barcelona, Spain. He has been a guest researcher at MACBA's Study Centre, and has worked as a digital photography consultant for the Landscape Observatory of Catalonia in the development of the Online Image Archive. Jon has curated group and solo exhibitions as co-founder of Widephoto, an independent platform which organised workshops, performances and self-publishing related events. He regularly guest lectures in European universities and his work has been internationally exhibited at El Círculo de Bellas Artes in Madrid, the University of Puerto Rico in San Juan, the Stadthaus in Ulm and La Capella in Barcelona among others.

Inioluwa Deborah Raji

is a researcher interested in topics of algorithmic auditing and evaluation. She has worked closely with the Algorithmic Justice League initiative on several award-winning projects to highlight cases of bias in computer vision. She has also worked with Google's Ethical AI team and been a research fellow at the Partnership on AI, at the AI Now Institute at New York University and at Mozilla working on various projects to operationalize ethical considerations in machine learning engineering practice.

Genevieve Fried

worked at New York University at the AI Now Institute, where she researched the social and policy implications of artificial intelligence. She has been involved in a number of policy and advocacy efforts around equitable, responsible, and accountable development and deployment of algorithms and is published in both academic and non-academic venues. A graduate of McGill University, she worked for several years as an artificial intelligence researcher and manager of the Reasoning and Learning Lab.

Dr. Heather Dewey-Hagborg

is an artist and biohacker who is interested in art as research and technological critique. Her controversial biopolitical art practice includes the project *Stranger Visions* in which she created portrait sculptures from analyses of genetic material (hair, cigarette butts, chewed up gum) collected in public places. Heather has shown work internationally at events and venues including the World Economic Forum, the Daejeon Biennale, the Guangzhou Triennial, and the Shenzhen Urbanism and Architecture Biennale, Transmediale, the Walker Center for Contemporary Art, the Philadelphia Museum of Art, and PS1 MOMA. Her work is held in public collections of the Centre Pompidou, the Victoria and Albert Museum, the Wellcome Collection, the Exploratorium, and the New York Historical Society, among others, and has been widely discussed in the media, from the New York Times and the BBC to Art Forum and Wired. Heather has a PhD in Electronic Arts from Rensselaer Polytechnic Institute. She is a visiting assistant professor of Interactive Media at NYU Abu Dhabi, an Artist-in-Residence at the Exploratorium, and is an affiliate of Data & Society. She is also a co-founder and co-curator of REFRESH, an inclusive and politically engaged collaborative platform at the intersection of Art, Science, and Technology.

Florian A. Schmidt

is a professor for Design and Media Theory at the University of Applied Sciences HTW Dresden. He holds a diploma in Communication Design from the Weissensee Academy of Art Berlin and a Ph.D. from the Royal College of Art in London. His doctoral thesis *Crowd Design* (Birkhäuser, 2017) is an analysis of the crowdsourcing of design as well as the design of crowdsourcing. He has published widely on the intersection of design, digital media and the future of work. His latest research reports are: *Digital Labour Markets in the Platform Economy* (FES, 2016); *Gig Work in Berlin* (City of Berlin, 2017); and *Crowdsourced Production of AI Training Data* (HBS, 2019). He was a speaker at conferences such as the Digital Labor Conference in New York, Reshaping Work in Amsterdam, transmediale and re:publica in Berlin. He has consulted committees on digital labour and the platform economy at the Deutsche Bundestag in Berlin as well as the EU in Brussels.

Sebastian Schmieg

Working in a wide range of media, including video and installation as well as lecture performance and delivery service, Sebastian Schmieg investigates the algorithmic circulation of images, texts, and bodies. He creates playful interventions that penetrate the shiny surfaces of our networked society and explore the realities that lie behind them. In particular, Schmieg focuses on outsourcing, algorithmic management, and artificial intelligence. Schmieg's work has been exhibited internationally at The Photographers' Gallery, London; Museum der bildenden Künste, Leipzig; Haus der elektronischen Künste, Basel; and Chronus Art Center, Shanghai, among others. He lives in Berlin and is a Professor of Interface Design at HTW Dresden.

xtine burrough

is a hybrid artist. She uses remix as a strategy for engaging networked audiences in critical participation at the intersection of media art and digital poetry. A Professor and Area Head of Design + Creative Practice in the School of Arts, Technology, and Emerging Communication at the University of Texas at Dallas, burrough is the Creative Director of LabSynthE, a laboratory for synthetic, electronic poetry. She has recently authored *Foundations of Digital Art and Design*, 2nd Edition and is co-editor of *The Routledge Handbook of Remix Studies and Digital Humanities*.

Sabrina Starnaman

researches socially-engaged literature, particularly Progressive Era (1880-1930) American texts about women's activism, urbanism, and disability that explores how activists remediated exploitative labor practices, racism, and poverty. Her work brings the voices of overlooked writers, particularly women writers, back into the public consciousness. Starnaman is an Associate Professor of Instruction of Literature and Director of Research for LabSynthE, a laboratory for synthetic, electronic poetry at the University of Texas at Dallas. burrough and Starnaman's collaborations are accessible on VisibleWomen.net.

Everest Pipkin

is a drawing and software artist from Central Texas, who produces intimate work with large data sets. Through the use of online archives, big data repositories, and other resources for digital information, they aim to reclaim the corporate Internet as a space that can be gentle, ecological, and personal. They hold a BFA from University of Texas at Austin, a MFA from Carnegie Mellon University, and have shown nationally and internationally at The Design Museum of London, The Texas Biennial, The XXI Triennale of Milan, The Photographers' Gallery of London, Center for Land Use Interpretation and others.

Alan Blackwell

is Professor of Interdisciplinary Design at the University of Cambridge. He worked in technology consultancies and corporate research centres as an artificial intelligence (AI) engineer during the 1990s, before undertaking a PhD in cognitive neuroscience. His recent research has studied alternative conceptions of AI from the perspective of indigenous peoples, and among low-income communities in sub-Saharan Africa. He is director of Cambridge Global Challenges, a strategic research initiative of the University dedicated to addressing the Sustainable Development Goals in the Global South.

Gaia Tedone

is a curator and researcher with an expansive interest in the technologies of image formation and online curatorial practices. She holds an MFA in Curating from Goldsmiths College, London (2008) and was a Curatorial Fellow of the Whitney Independent Study Programme, New York (2011). Gaia is completing her PhD at the Centre for the Study of the Networked Image, London South Bank University with a practice-based research entitled 'Curating The Networked Image: Circulation, Commodification, Computation'. Her project explores the increasingly hybrid understanding of the curatorial function online, as shaped by the convergence of different professional fields and in light of existing conditions of online image searching, reproduction and circulation. Her recent publications on the topic include: 'Networked Co-Curation: An Exploration of the Socio-Technical Specificities of Online Curation' with Annet Dekker, *Arts*, 2019, 8(3), 86; 'Human-Algorithmic Curation: Curating with or against the Algorithm?' *Conference Proceedings of the 7th Conference on Computation, Communication, Aesthetics & X*, Milan, Fabbrica del Vapore, July 2019; 'Tracing Networked Images: an Emerging Method for Online Curation', *Journal of Media Practice*, 2017, 18:1, 51-62.

Nicolas Malevé

is an artist, programmer and data activist. He has recently completed his PhD at London South Bank University, as part of a collaboration with The Photographers' Gallery where he initiated the project Variations on a Glance (2015-2018), a series of workshops on the photographic elaboration of computer vision. He is currently a postdoc researcher at the School of Communication and Culture at Aarhus University, supported by a grant from the Novo Nordisk Foundation (NNF21OC0068539).

This book is published
by The Photographers'
Gallery digital programme
in 2023.

Title: A Cat, a Dog, a Microwave...
Subtitle: Cultural Practices
and Politics of Image Datasets.
Editors: Nicolas Malevé
and Ioanna Zouli.

ISBN: 978-1-9163487-2-1

Contributing authors:
Florian A. Schmidt, Alan Blackwell,
xtine burrough & Sabrina
Starnaman, Geoff Cox, Heather
Dewey-Hagborg, Genevieve
Fried & Deborah Raji, Nicolas
Malevé and Sebastian Schmieg,
Nicolas Malevé, Everest Pipkin,
Gaia Tedone, Jon Uriarte,
Ioanna Zouli and Katrina Sluis.

Contributing artists:
xtine burrough & Sabrina
Starnaman, Heather
Dewey-Hargborg,
Anna Ridler, The
Scandinavian Institute for
Computational Vandalism,
Sebastian Schmieg, Philipp Schmitt,
Mimi Onuoha and Everest Pipkin.

End papers illustrations
by Nicolas Malevé.

Graphic design:
Oficina de Disseny
– Ariadna Serrahima,
Diego Bustamante.

Copy editor: Arieh Frosh
Proofreader: Beth Bramich
Publication Coordinator: Jon Uriarte
Printer: Aprograf, Barcelona

Special thanks to Philipp
Schmitt, Martin Steininger,
Anna Dannemann, Anna
Ridler, Montserrat Gonzalez,
Sam Mercer, Mimi Onuoha,
Tim Bowditch, Kate Elliott.

Every effort has been made to
contact copyright holders and
to obtain their permission for
the use of copyright material.
If inadvertent infringement
has occurred please contact
the publisher.

© 2023 Texts: the respective authors
© 2023 Images: the respective artists

This publication is licensed
under a Creative Commons
Attribution-NonCommercial
-ShareAlike 4.0 International
Licence (CC BY-NC-SA 4.0).
To view a copy of this license,
visit https://creativecommons.
org/licenses/by-nc-sa/4.0/

First edition, 2023
The Photographers' Gallery
is a registered charity
funded by Arts Council
England Registered
charity no 262548
The Photographers' Gallery
16-18 Ramillies Street
London W1F 7LW
www.tpg.org.uk

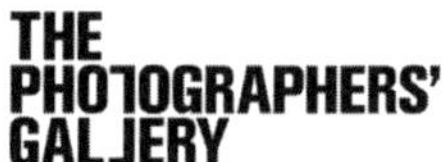

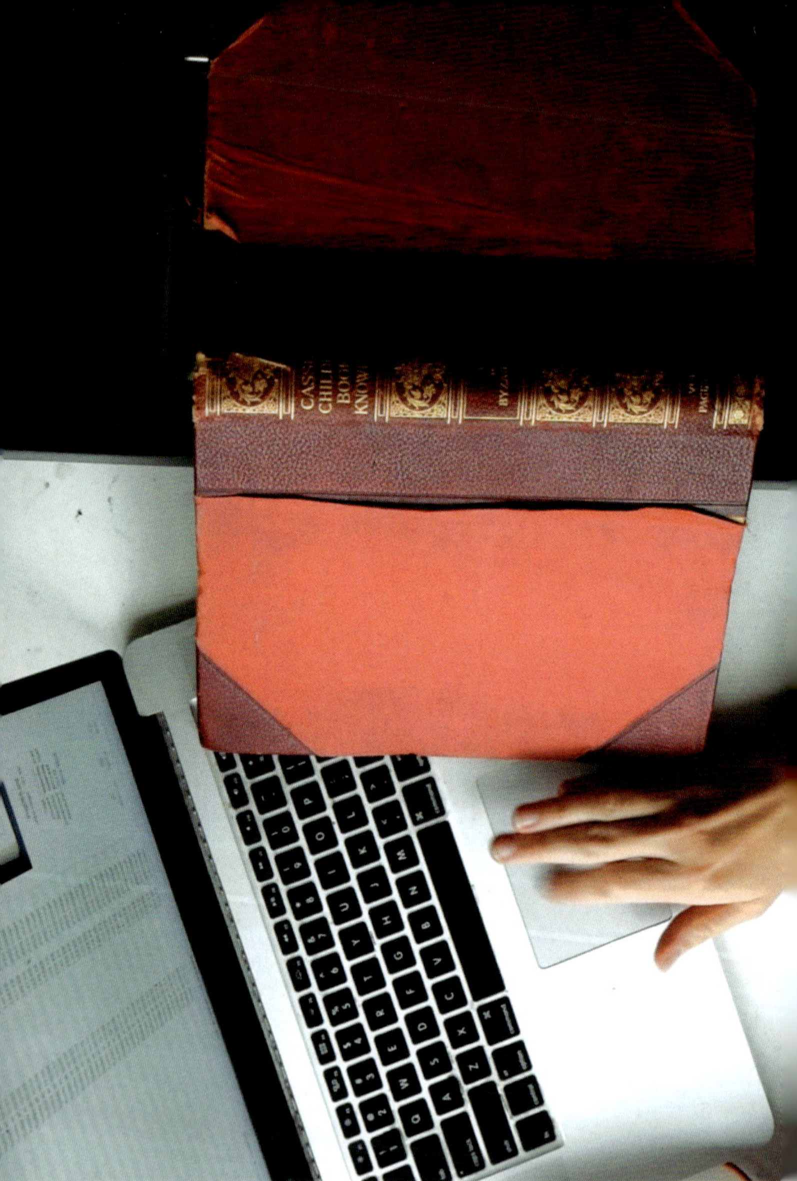

IMG 1: Still from Anna Ridler's 'Laws of Ordered Form',
presented on TPG Media Wall in 2020 as part
of the Data/Set/Match programme.

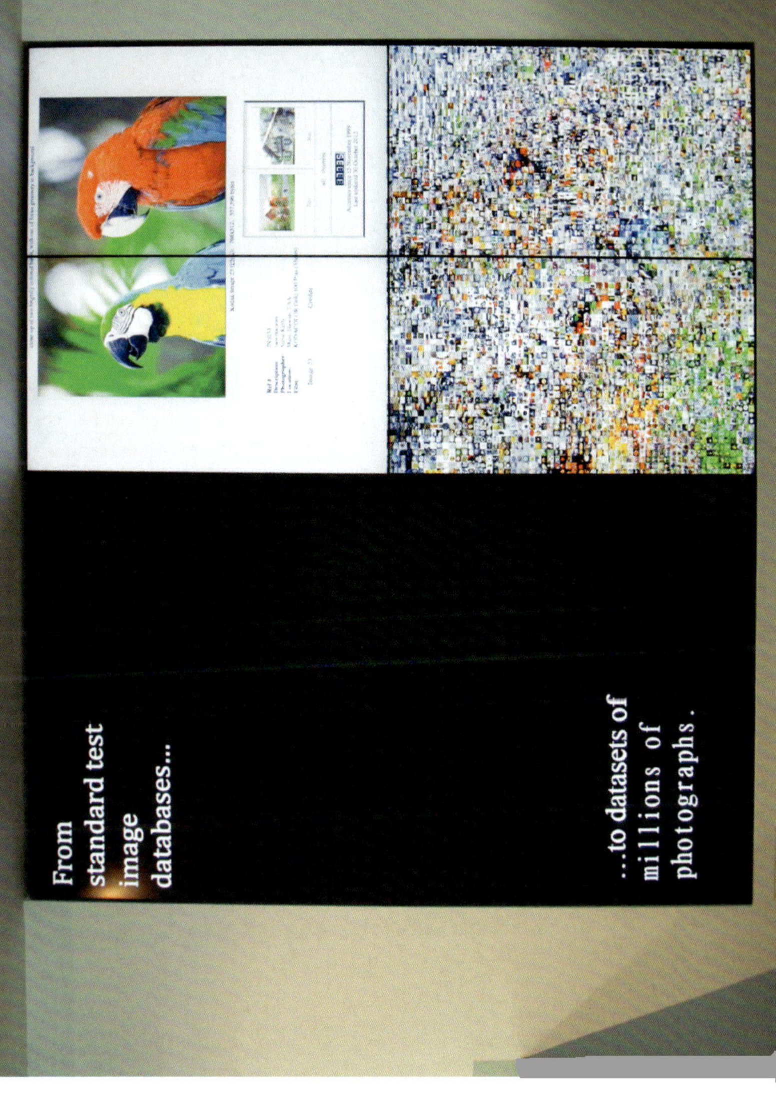

IMG 2: Installation image from TPG Media Wall
presenting an introductory video essay to Data/Set/Match.
© Kate Elliott

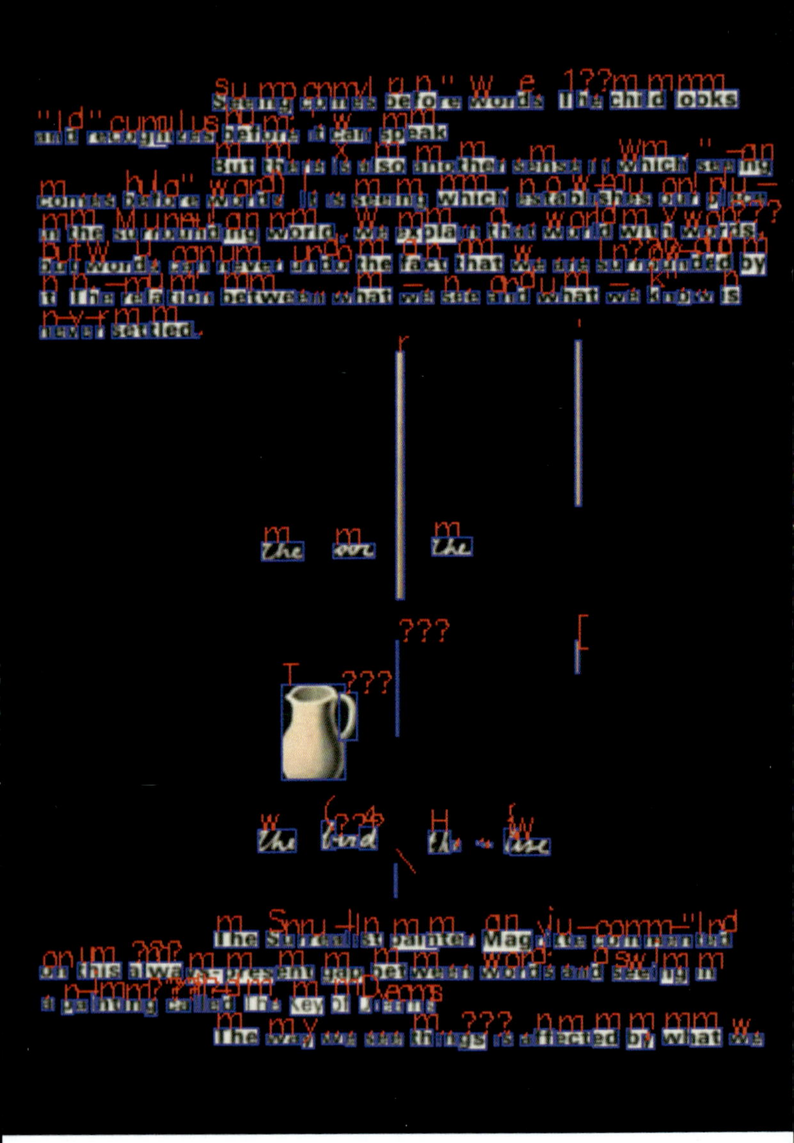

Seeing comes before words. The child looks and recognizes before it can speak.

But there is also another sense in which seeing comes before words. It is seeing which establishes our place in the surrounding world; we explain that world with words, but words can never undo the fact that we are surrounded by it. The relation between what we see and what we know is never settled.

the   our   the

the   bird   the   use

The Surrealist painter Magritte commented on this always-present gap between words and seeing in a painting called The Key of Dreams.

The way we see things is affected by what we

IMG 3: The 'Ways of Seeing' book cover image seen through an optical character recognition programme. Created by the Scandinavian Institute for Computational Vandalism.

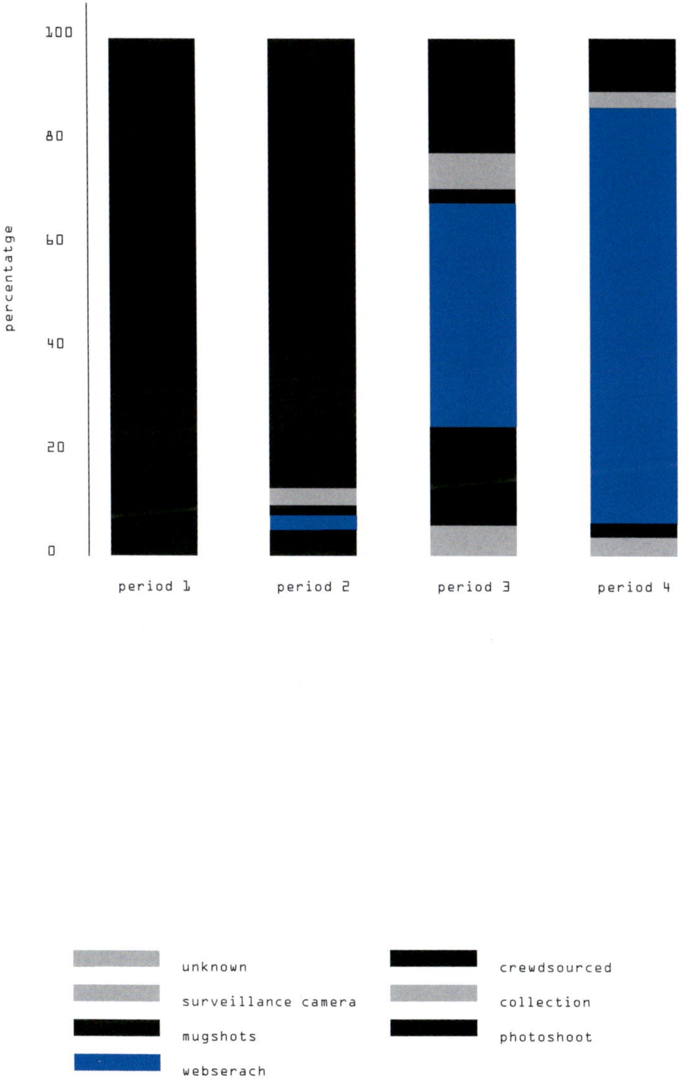

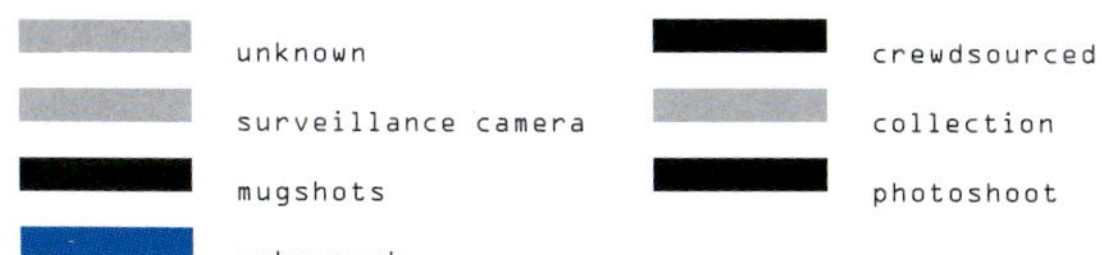

IMG 4: Summary of proportion of dataset sources for each period.

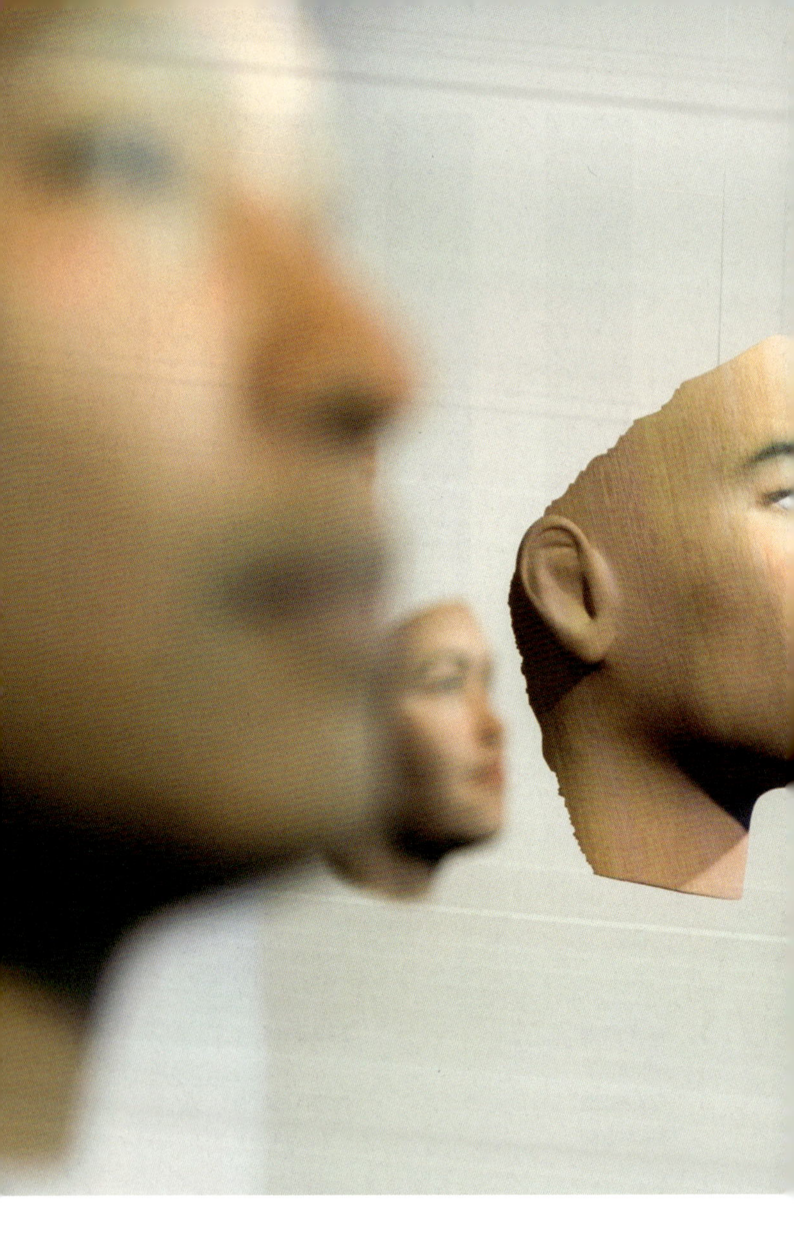

IMG 5: Still from the work 'Probably Chelsea' (2017)
© Heather Dewey-Hagborg and Chelsea E. Manning.

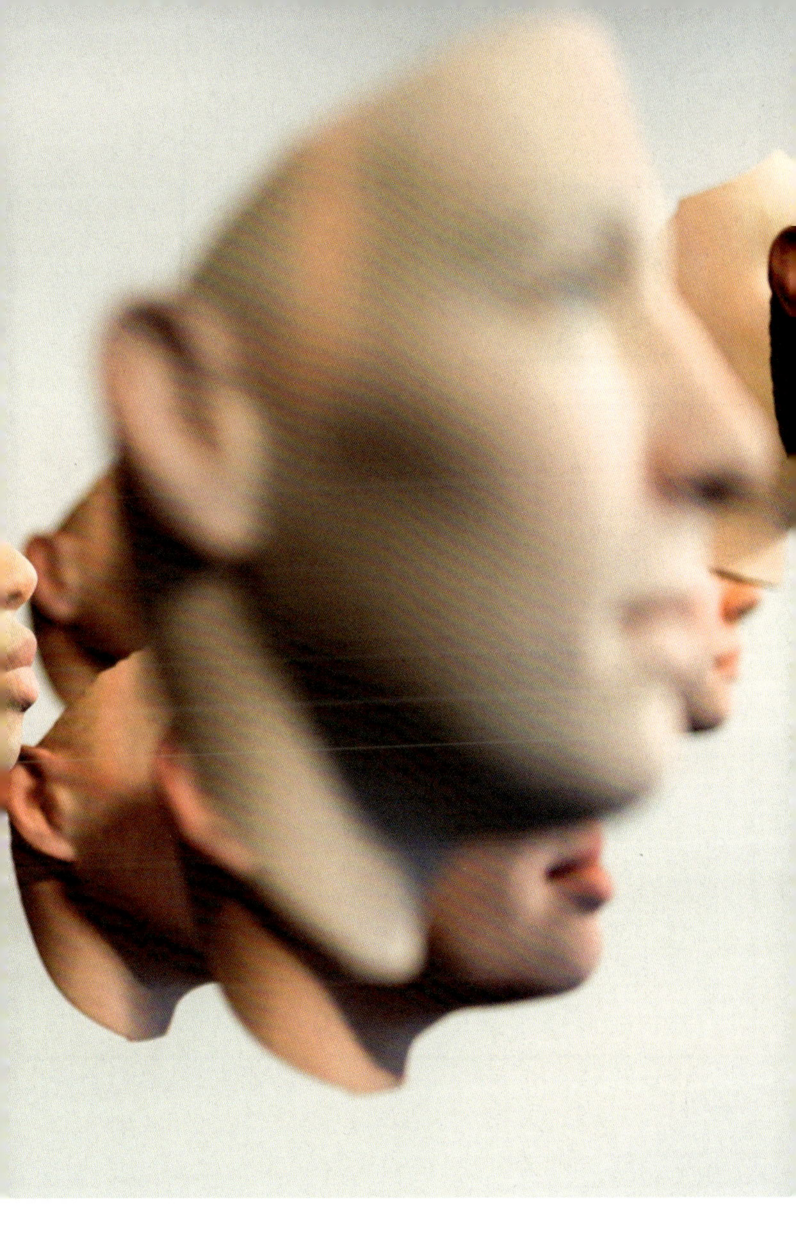

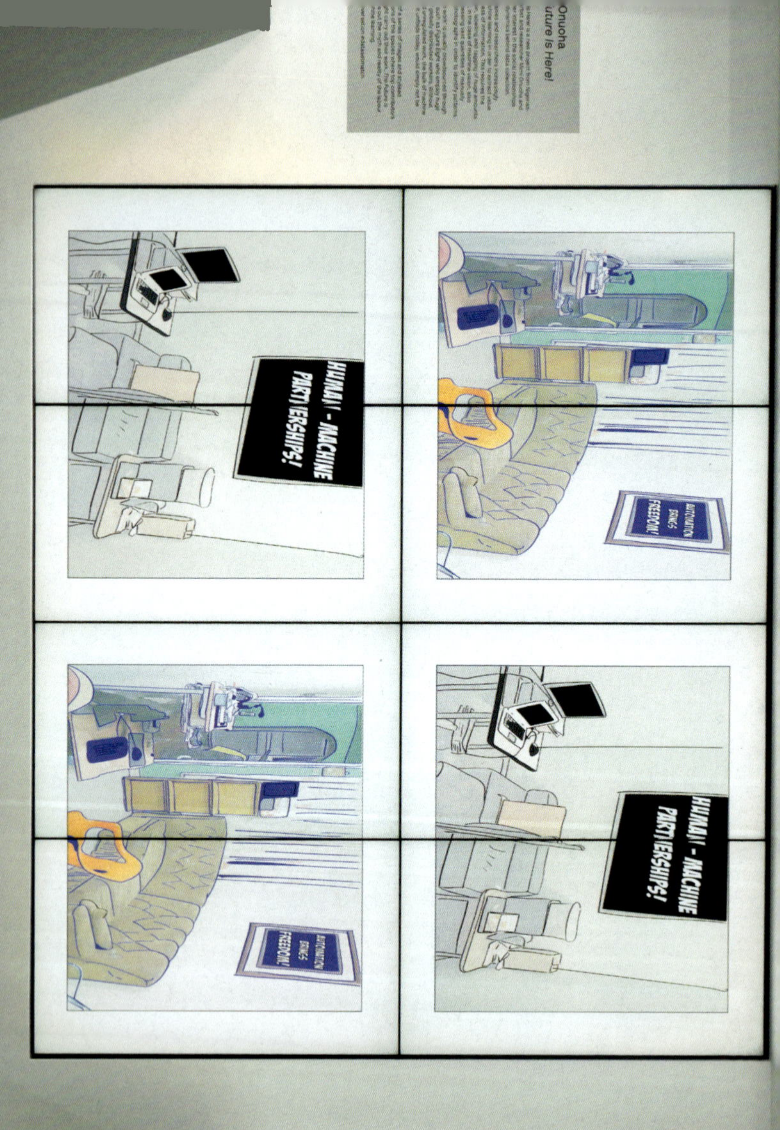

IMG 6 / 7: Installation image from Mimi Onuoha's
'The Future Is Here!' shown on TPG Media Wall
from December 2019 until January 2020.

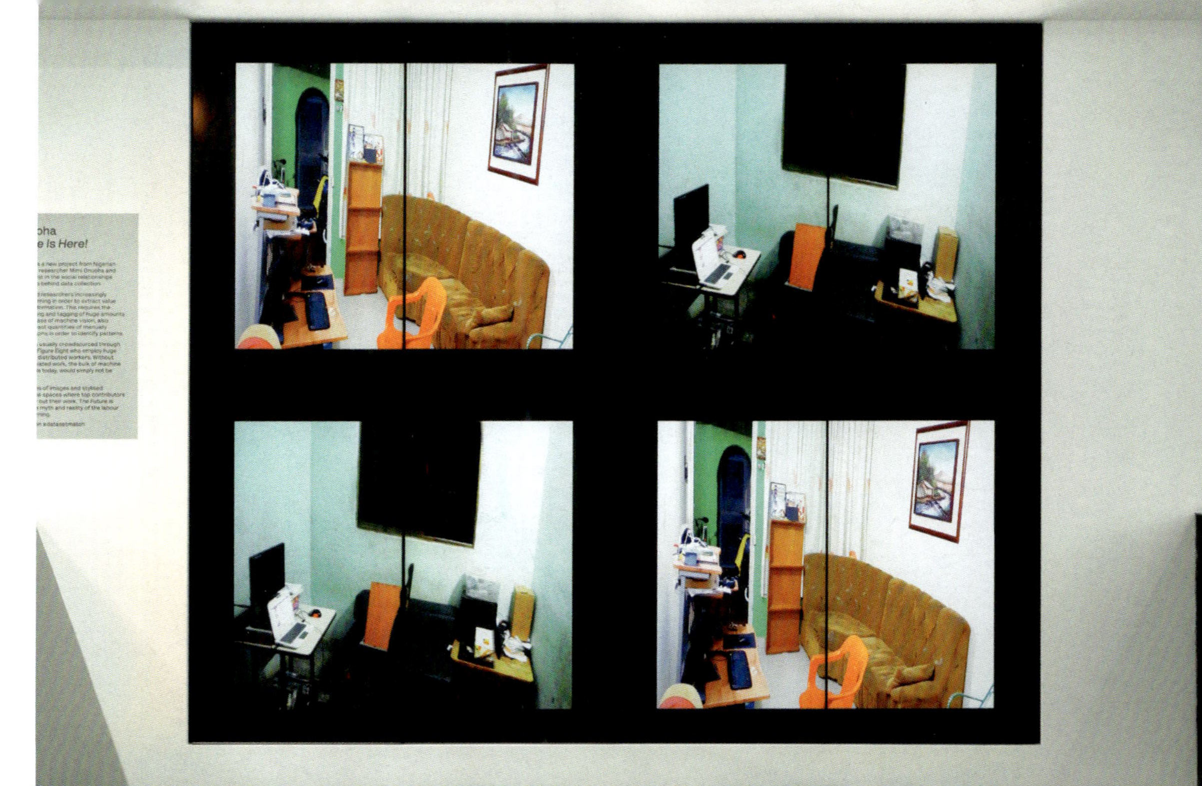
…oha
…e Is Here!

…s a new project from Nigerian
…researcher Mimi Onuoha and
…st in the social relationships
…behind data collection.

…d researchers increasingly
…ning in order to extract value
…formation. This requires the
…ng and tagging of huge amounts
…se of machine vision, also
…ast quantities of manually
…ons in order to identify patterns

…usually crowdsourced through
…Figure Eight who employ huge
…distributed workers. Without
…ated work, the bulk of machine
…s today, would simply not be

…s of images and stylised
…e spaces where top contributors
…out their work. The Future is
…myth and reality of the labour
…ning.

…a datasetmaton

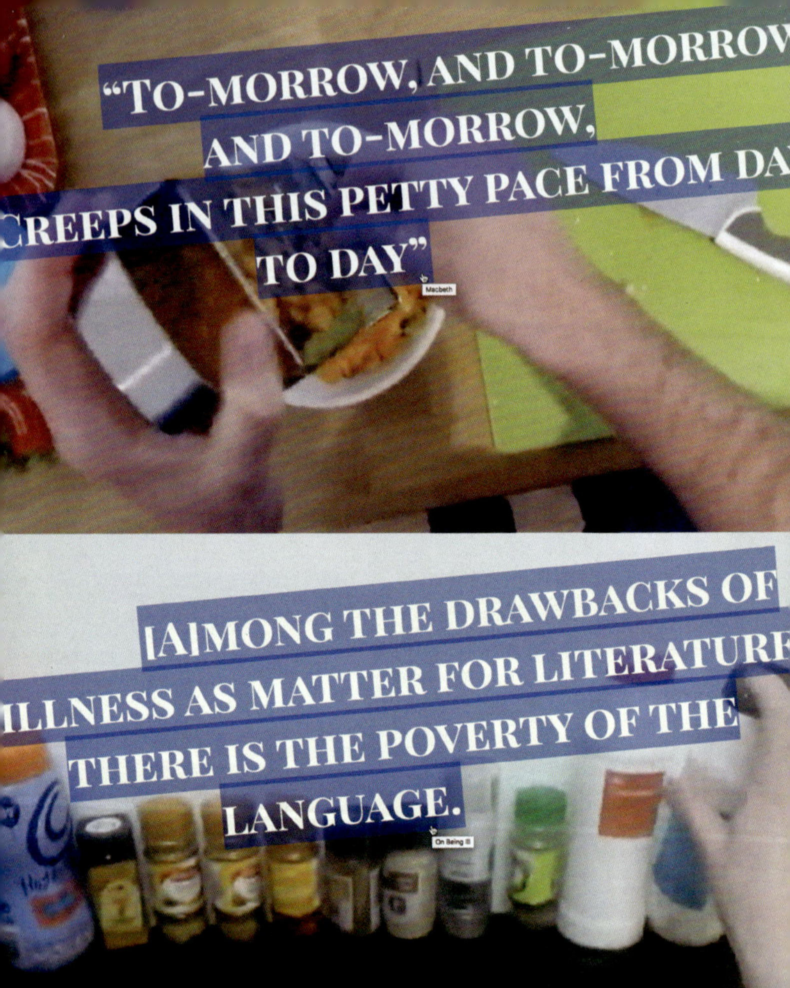

IMG 8: 'Epic Hand Washing in a Time of Lost Narratives', burrough and Starnaman, screenshot, March 2020. Videos from Epic Kitchens, quote from William Shakespeare,'Macbeth'.

IMG 9: 'Epic Hand Washing in a Time of Lost Narratives', burrough and Starnaman, screenshot, March 2020. Videos from Epic Kitchens, quote from Virginia Woolf, 'On Being Ill'.

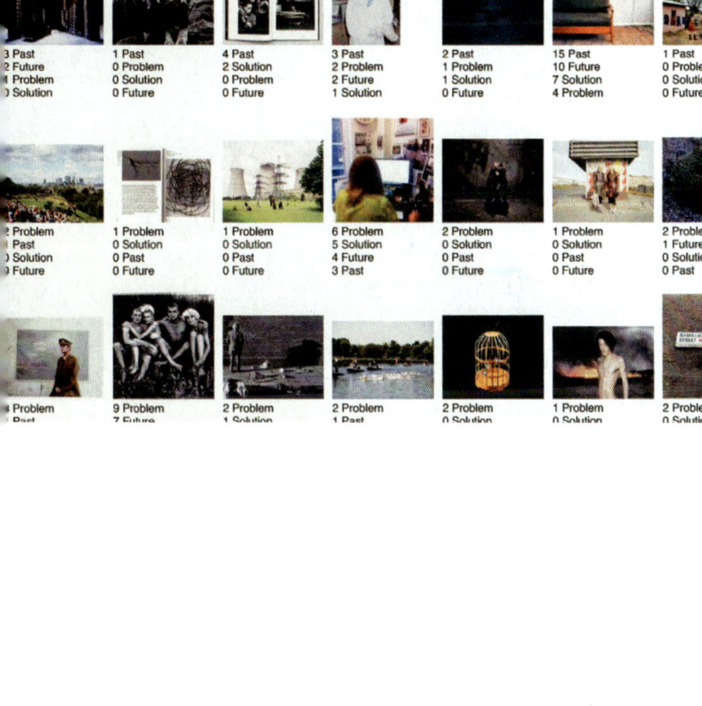

Solution
0 Future

1 Past
0 Problem
0 Solution
0 Future

2 Past
0 Problem
0 Solution
0 Future

4 Past
1 Problem
1 Future
0 Solution

2 Past
1 Future
0 Problem
0 Solution

1 Past
0 Problem
0 Solution
0 Future

1 Past
0 Problem
0 Solution
0 Future

2 Past
1 Problem
1 Future
0 Solution

2 Past
0 P
0 S
0 F

2 Past
0 Problem
0 Solution
0 Future

2 Past
1 Solution
0 Problem
0 Future

48 Past
39 Future
27 Problem
26 Solution

2 Past
0 Problem
0 Solution
0 Future

3 Past
0 Problem
0 Solution
0 Future

1 Past
0 Problem
0 Solution
0 Future

2 Past
1 Problem
1 Future
0 Solution

7 P
3 S
2 F
1 P

3 Past
2 Future
1 Problem
0 Solution

1 Past
0 Problem
0 Solution
0 Future

4 Past
2 Solution
0 Problem
0 Future

3 Past
2 Problem
2 Future
1 Solution

2 Past
1 Problem
1 Solution
0 Future

15 Past
10 Future
7 Solution
4 Problem

1 Past
0 Problem
0 Solution
0 Future

2 P
1 P
1 F
0 S

2 Problem
1 Past
0 Solution
0 Future

1 Problem
0 Solution
0 Past
0 Future

1 Problem
0 Solution
0 Past
0 Future

6 Problem
5 Solution
4 Future
3 Past

2 Problem
0 Solution
0 Past
0 Future

1 Problem
0 Solution
0 Past
0 Future

2 Problem
1 Future
0 Solution
0 Past

5 P
1 P
1 F
0 S

1 Problem
1 Past

9 Problem
7 Future

2 Problem
1 Solution

2 Problem
1 Past

2 Problem
0 Solution

1 Problem
0 Solution

2 Problem
0 Solution

2 P
0 S

IMG 10: An excerpt from the dataset created
by the audience's participation in 'Decision Space'.
© Sebastian Schmieg

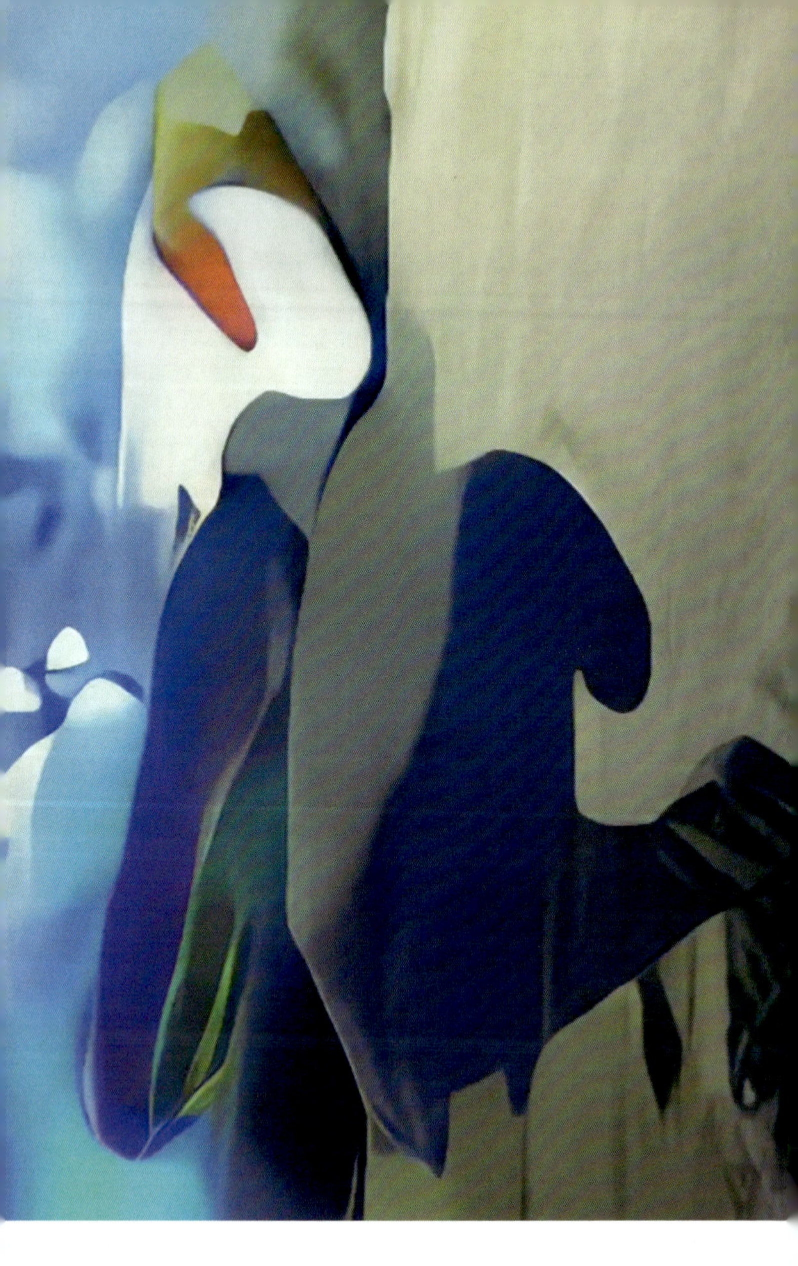

IMG 11: Screenshot from Everest Pipkin's 'Lacework' (2020).

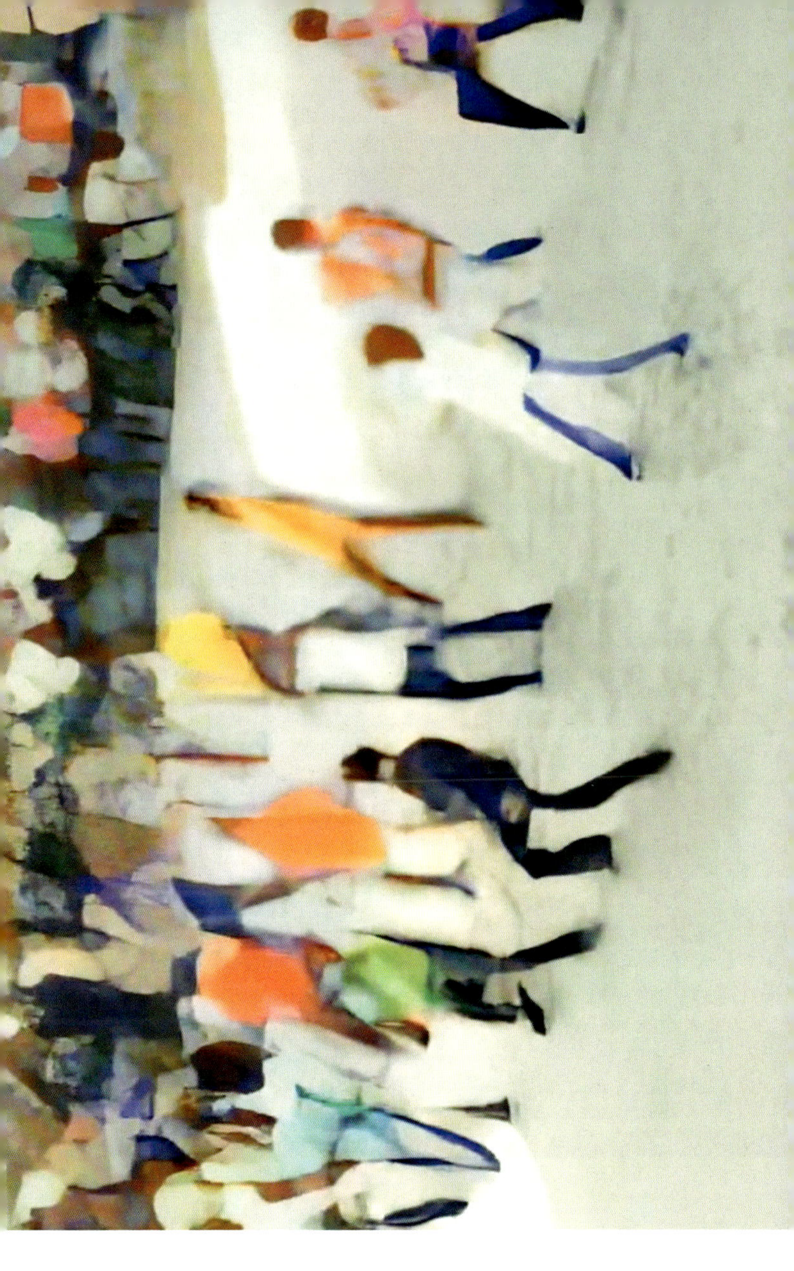

IMG 12: Screenshot from Everest Pipkin's 'Lacework' (2020).

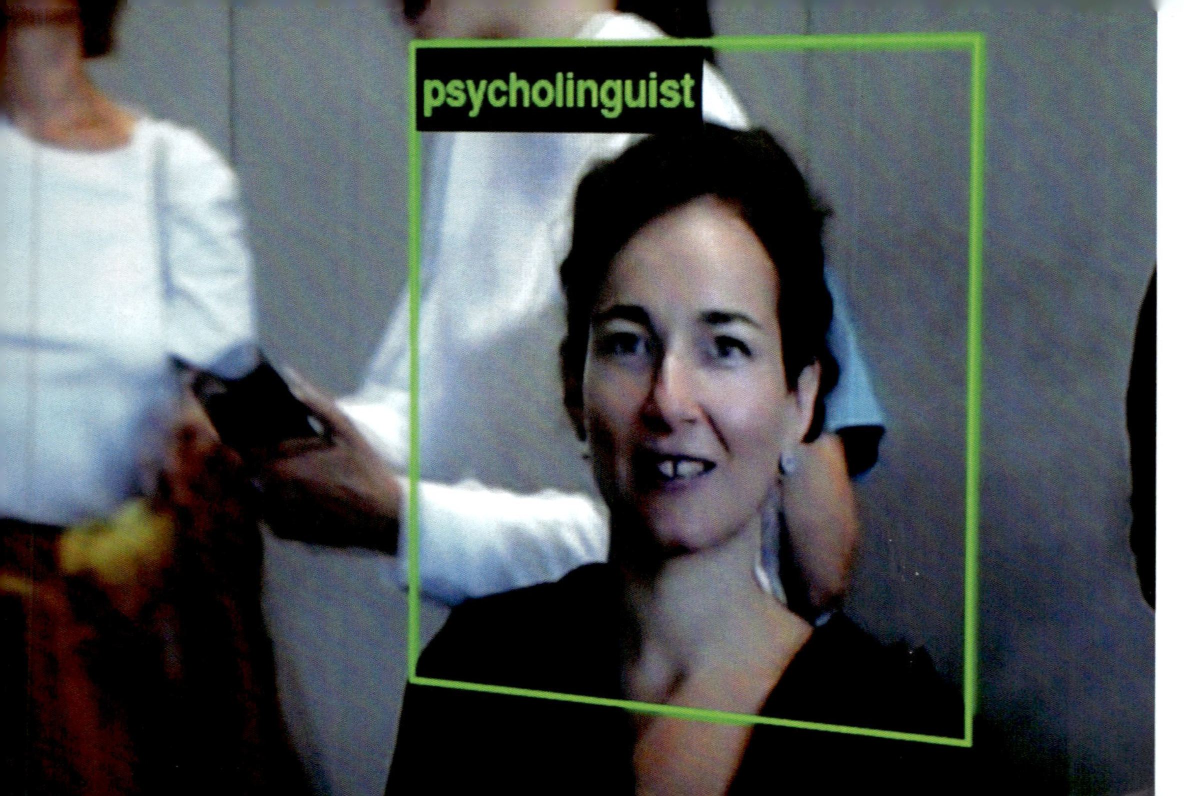

IMG 13: The author (Gaia Tedone) at the installation of 'ImageNet Roulette'. Video still from Alessandro Sambini.